The Rainmaker

The Rainmaker

Start-Up to Conglomerate

Business Success in a Hostile Global Environment

Jacques Magliolo

BEP BUSINESS EXPERT PRESS

The Rainmaker: Start-Up to Conglomerate
Copyright © Business Expert Press, LLC, 2019.

First published in 2019 by
Business Expert Press, LLC
222 East 46th Street, New York, NY 10017
www.businessexpertpress.com

ISBN-13: 978-1-94999-103-1 (paperback)
ISBN-13: 978-1-94999-104-8 (e-book)

Business Expert Press Entrepreneurship and Small Business Management Collection

Collection ISSN: 1946-5653 (print)
Collection ISSN: 1946-5661 (electronic)

Cover and interior design by S4Carlisle Publishing Services Private Ltd., Chennai, India

First edition: 2019

10 9 8 7 6 5 4 3 2 1

Printed in the United States of America.

Dedication

*A word of thanks and gratitude to all angels who have helped
entrepreneurs find their dreams and succeed, especially those who
went beyond the call of duty.*

Abstract

According to Bloomberg, 8 out of 10 entrepreneurs who start businesses fail within the first 18 months. Despite being shocking and true, this is mostly preventable. Many entrepreneurs cite undercapitalization at the outset of starting a business as a major reason for failure. That is truly a poor excuse—there is no need to be undercapitalized in a world where over US$1 trillion was invested in new projects in 2016—and today almost twice that number of funds are available since crowdfunding took off.

Despite the flow of international funds, many entrepreneurs have an unwillingness to see that they have poorly structured companies, no valuation, and lack of cohesive strategy. Not taking advice from independent professionals becomes the noose from which entrepreneurs hang their businesses.

These are some of the more simple and basic reasons for failure.

The Rainmaker is an individual who can assist entrepreneurs to succeed past that 18-month barrier by helping them structure and run a company that meets ultimate best practice solutions and systems that are realistic and competitively better than peers.

The Rainmaker surrounds himself or herself with a small team of professionals to carry out necessary and pertinent corporate requirements as determined and instructed by *The Rainmaker*.

The Rainmaker is a combination of trouble shooter, advisor, mentor, and financier.

Keywords

rainmaker; entrepreneur; survival; directives; corporate; legal; feasibilities; strategic tools; startups; tools; finances; forecasts; presentation; overtrading

Contents

What Is a Rainmaker?

Over centuries, the classical definition has evolved to refer to someone who can call on nature and all its elements, to serve a greater good, as *A Rainmaker*. Originally, the meaning was more simplistic, and a rainmaker was someone who could call on the rain gods to quench the thirst of drought-stricken areas, but it then evolved to refer to a person who could call on gods to resolve any problem, no matter how complex or seemingly impossible.

In modern economic history, this definition migrated to financial markets to refer to a rainmaker as a master of manifestation—someone who could identify problems and bring solutions. At first, it strictly referred to bringing finance to cash-strapped organizations but more recently to resolving complex problems that could bring financial ruin to companies. Some experts refer to this as *making it rain money!*

I believe that the original cosmic definition should prevail, even if used in the context of financial markets. So when someone uses powers of deduction and logic to make it rain money or success in any form, and when that power to create is used with integrity and honesty, then everyone must benefit. In fact, the opposite is also true. When this ability and skill is used for selfish or personal gains only, everyone ultimately suffers.

Rainmakers thus bring back to life companies that have temporarily faulted, cannot raise capital, or seem to be staggering toward financial oblivion. They do this by working with what the current situation is compared to what it should be. For instance, if a factory has made 1,000 gadgets, but it should have made 2,000 gadgets, then the question starts with *Why*. Entrepreneurs who adopt the same philosophical stance will find that they are more focused and, in turn, so too are their companies.

Word of Advice

A goal without a plan is just a wish.
Antoine de Saint-Exupéry (1900–1944)
French writer, poet, aristocrat, journalist, and pioneering aviator

The following should become part of your everyday personal and business life:

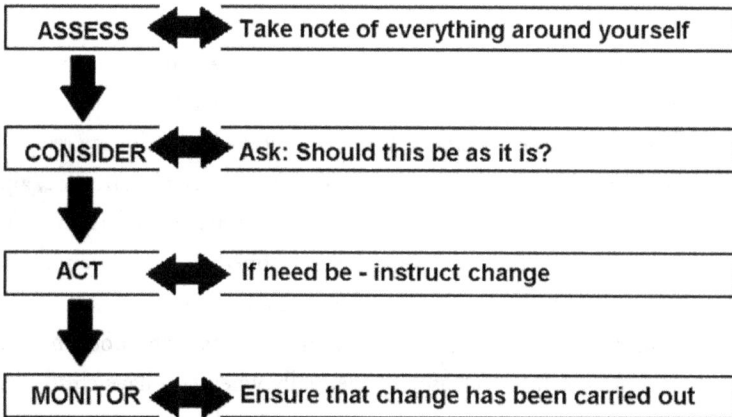

ASSESS ◄──►	Take note of everything around yourself

⬇

CONSIDER ◄──►	Ask: Should this be as it is?

⬇

ACT ◄──►	If need be - instruct change

⬇

MONITOR ◄──►	Ensure that change has been carried out

NOTE:
* DON'T LET ANYTHING STAGNATE
* SMALL THINGS CAN BECOME IMPOSSIBLE TO
  FIX LATER ON

Stated differently:

- Always be aware of your business environment, including changing trends, competitors, pricing and accessibility to products and services, and your (and your business's) ability to finance current business operations and possible future expansion.
- Consider what problems have occurred (or could occur), and strategize to immediately resolve *all* issues and concerns before they become serious impediments to the smooth running of your business.

- Then take immediate action to ensure that such issues have been resolved.
- Finally, ensure that actions are in place to keep such problems from reoccurring.

This book is designed to help you set up a solid business foundation and then to ensure that you continue to maintain that structure through well-planned strategies. You also need to be effective in your implementation of plans to achieve corporate objectives and goals. It is also pointless to achieve goals at the expense of financial stability.

After all, dozens of economic journals around the world in recent years have stated that entrepreneurship is the most prevalent source of global wealth, today and increasingly so in the future. It has been documented that entrepreneurs are found to accumulate wealth at a greater rate than in any previous decade. This highlights expert views that the growth of global wealth is now being driven by specifically small businesses.

In fact, wealth is being created twice as quickly in developing regions, such as Asia Pacific, Africa, South America, the former Eastern Bloc, and Middle East, where it takes such individuals an average of 12 years to accumulate wealth, compared to more developed markets such as the United States and Europe, where it takes an average of 28 years.

Starting a business is thus less risky than doomsayers proclaim, but the rate of success does increase exponentially when you have created an effective corporate structure to mirror international best-practice trends.

This comes with experience, skill, and dedication.

About the Book

Target market: novice to professional entrepreneurs in any country and of any magnitude.

- **Aim of the book:** to assist entrepreneurs in three ways:
    - To create the most efficient and profitable corporate structure from the outset.
    - To outline rules on how to immediately fix problems when they arise.
    - How to expand your business and raise critical capital, while not depleting current cash flows. Remember that mergers and acquisitions take time, effort, and serious cash reserves, so don't ignore your current customers, staff, and operations. The aim of this book is definitely not to regurgitate theories and common practices outlined in thousands of business and self-help books.
        - As such, I aim to guide you to develop your own set of rules, which suit your personal circumstances, whatever your product or services may be and wherever in the world you may operate.

This is a book on how to structure any business to build wealth, based on a foundation of knowledge and business/corporate discipline. This book covers the basics to ultimately run a business in the global markets. It is a culmination of theory and practical application taken from my 30-year track record as economist and corporate advisor.

The aim is simple—to demystify the complexities that make up business and corporate markets around the world. It is written with some pertinent lists, observations, and comments. It is important to note that some chapters concentrate on financing the company, from start-up to established firms.

Many MBA business textbooks are great for anyone looking to build knowledge of complex theories, but there is a vast gap in such books to develop an effective business that is prepared for any eventuality, whether from staff, fellow directors, clients, suppliers, and so on.

In today's digital world, filled with online business courses, training programs, and free workshops, there is no reason why you cannot build a solid and practical foundation of knowledge. How you apply this knowledge is up to you.

Now, let's get to it.

At the outset, it must be noted that—according to Bloomberg—80 percent of entrepreneurs who start businesses fail within the first 18 months. While this statistic may be shocking and certainly true, it is, nevertheless, mostly preventable.

Many entrepreneurs cite undercapitalization at the outset of starting a business as a major reason for failure. This is truly a poor excuse. These businessmen and businesswomen should have been better prepared, with focused due diligence and required funds. In fact, there is today no need to be undercapitalized in a world where over US$1 trillion has been invested in new projects since 2016—and today almost twice that amount of funds is available since crowdfunding took off.

What is even more sad is the occasions when all prelaunch studies have been done properly, but greed and lack of a coordinated plan still see failure. I have seen entrepreneurs succeed in raising the funds that they have assessed would be required until profits kick in, only to run out of these within an extremely short time. The fact is that these entrepreneurs either didn't follow their business and strategy plans or ignored advisors and key staff as to spending patterns. Entrepreneurial success is never merely a wish list, nor is it a desire to be free of obligation and boring routine. The idea of being your own boss is wonderful, except that your responsibilities should never be taken lightly, as you have effectively become accountable to paying, among others, staff, clients, and suppliers. Creating and running a business takes dedication, commitment, and, more importantly, focus.

And doing things right the first time.

Many entrepreneurs have too much pride to surround themselves with experts—and, as we know, *pride comes before a fall.* Such pride prevents entrepreneurs from all walks of life across all countries from taking pertinent and truly relevant advice from professionals, which often perpetuates the myth that the success and prosperity of the company is inextricably linked to the persona of the founder. While this may have been true in the distant past, companies today are weighed down by multiple rules, guidelines, and legislation. Without a sound understanding of all these variables, or an unwillingness to see that your corporate structure does not meet true transparency and governance, personality will be swamped by red tape and poor judgment. Consequently, failure justifies statistics.

In reality, you want your business to be perceived as both professional and effective. In addition, these are qualities that add significantly to the value of your business. In listed companies, the share price multiplied by the amount of issued shares tells you what the company is worth, but in an unlisted company the value is based on profits, competitive edge, and its effectiveness in today's environment to achieve forecasts. So a lack of cohesive corporate, marketing, and financial strategies becomes the noose from which businesses come to an inevitable end.

These are some of the simpler and basic reasons for failure. Not knowing when you have reached your limit as an efficient and effective leader often results in loss of business—from finance to operations to marketing.

This brings us to the title and thus the focus of this book. So, what is *The Rainmaker* in the context of this book? *The Rainmaker* is an individual who can assist you to succeed past that 18-month'barrier by helping you structure and run your company to meet ultimate best-practice solutions and systems, which are realistic and competitively better than your peers'.

They do this by using three basic methods:

- **First, *The Rainmaker* ensures that you have the proper structure with which to start your business**: Do you comply with legal, government, social, and environmental guidelines and statutes?
- **Second, *The Rainmaker* assists you to fix problems when they arise** and to ensure that the company strategically meets continually and rapidly changing consumer, economic, and market conditions and trends.
- **Third, *The Rainmaker* should ensure that you and your company do not stagnate.** In other words, you should not stand

still—profits should grow, productivity should improve, and the organization should become larger and more efficient. A business must continue to grow and diversify, while balancing cashflow requirements, demand and supply of goods and services, and communication between directors, staff, and customers.

I define a rainmaker as someone who is able to surround himself or herself with a small team of professionals so that they can establish a solid foundation for a start-up, quickly fix, coordinate recovery, finance, and advise on how to run a profitable business.

The Rainmaker is, in my opinion, a combination of troubleshooter, advisor, and mentor. In truth, *The Rainmaker* simply uses a combination of corporate knowledge, experience in turning theory into practice, and logic in comparing *what is* with *what should be.*

Despite horrendous statistics, this is an exciting journey for anyone who desires to create a business that will make a difference to employees and the environment alike. While unsubstantiated, the following facts are interesting: for every person employed, four additional people are supported in first world countries and as many as 15 people in developing countries.

My goal in writing this book is thus to make the process of running and financing your company, across as many diverse industries as I possibly can, easier and relatively pain free. It is my desire that you, no matter the size of your business, use this book and its principles to achieve your goals for your staff, directors, and yourself but also to exert a positive influence on the community, such as creating employment and thus reducing hardship.

Whatever your question, feel free to contact me via e-mail.

Jacques Magliolo
jsrmagliolo@gmail.com
https://jmagliolo.blog
2019

Acknowledgments

Special thanks to those rare souls who helped and mentored me diligently and patiently over the past 30 years. These include, among many others, Dr. Le Mont, Prof. Lloyd, Dr. Le Roux, Dr. Bruton, Adv. Miller, Steven Itzikowitz, Clive Miller, David Raw, and stockbroker Date Line.

CHAPTER 1

Introducing the Power Entrepreneur

Let me state that this is not strictly a textbook on business and how to raise funds. There are literally thousands of such books available worldwide, many free to download. If you need some assistance, send me an e-mail, and I will help you find information pertinent to your specific needs.

The Rainmaker is simply a menu of factors that you need to take extreme care and cognizance of to create a company that you will be proud of and achieve success for your customers, staff, the environment within which you operate, and, of course, for you and your partners.

In addition, to achieve your goals, whatever these may be, the business needs to be profitable, cash flush, and progressive for today and for the long term. Stated differently, in an environment that is highly, and at times, cruelly competitive, you need to drive innovation hard, be progressive in every facet of your business, and ensure that your company services and products are continually in demand. You have to accomplish these, while balancing people, money, and time. This is by no means an easy task to achieve.

Let's start with one pertinent and basic fact.

You need to draft a business plan. I am not suggesting that you have an expensive document that you ultimately never use. I am advising you to have a working document that is both a strategy and a plan for you and your business for today and the future. This should include, among others, goals and milestones. Some decades ago, my personal business mentor in stockbroking likened a business plan to a shopping list.

I think that the analogy is important, so I will repeat it here.

- **Scenario 1:** Imagine going shopping with a limited amount of funds and no shopping list.
- **Scenario 2:** Imagine going shopping with a limited amount of funds and a poorly thought-out shopping list.
- **Scenario 3:** Imagine going shopping with a limited amount of funds and a well-thought-out shopping list.

In scenario 1, you are likely to end up buying goods that you don't actually require, forgetting the more critical ones. In business, Imagine forgetting to buy fuel for your delivery trucks or a building construction company not purchasing cement. At the time, I said to my mentor that these were obvious purchases and, as such, I wouldn't forget—with or without a business plan.

He just smiled and said,

Maybe so, but without proper information, you could buy too much or too little cement. Either way, your business would come to a standstill. In the former, you wouldn't have enough cash to buy other material to finish the project (wooden beams, doors, and bricks, etc.), and in the latter, your project would come to a grinding halt very quickly.

In scenario 2, simply put—you could end up buying material that you may only need later in the project, while not buying the more currently pertinent materials. In the last example, you would be able to—over the years—home in on required materials and expenses as they are required.

In reality, a business plan is a strategy document, which should outline the responsibilities of key staff and directors. It should have deliverables and costings attached. At that stage, I was pretty naïve and said, "Surely, a business plan is private? Inserting competitively sensitive information in a document is not wise."

It is thus important to differentiate the specific uses of a business plan. In the first instance, a business plan is a strategy document for your board of directors. Secondly, parts of the document can be used for marketing and profiles, and, finally, it can be used to raise capital.

As such, the only way to achieve the various uses is to write a business plan in independent sections that can be removed for various purposes. While textbooks cite dozens of pertinent rules that entrepreneurs need to adhere to and—as stated so often—document in a business plan, there are actually also personality traits that are as important as dry facts. I will set these out more comprehensively in later chapters.

In the meantime, look at just four basic lessons by which many successful entrepreneurs live by, whether documented or not.

Our Starting Point—Four Lessons

- The first is that **complacency** in a world that is hostile and hungry to take your success away from you is detrimental to your financial health. Competitors, both new and experienced, will lure your skilled staff away with better financial packages, copy your products and services at lower prices, and undertake marketing campaigns aimed at stealing market share away from you.
  - I am not saying that their lower priced products will be better than yours, but in a world of personal financial stress, many buyers will try the new product.
- Second, **hesitation** to be innovative with current products and services or to expand your business into new yet related products could see your company stagnate and move into inevitable disbandment as better products enter the market at lower costs.
- Third, in a continually changing world of legislation and corporate rules and guidelines, ensure that you are focused. Ask yourself, "Is my plan properly structured to be effective from the first day, and can I stay ahead of competitors, both local and foreign?"
- Lastly, your company should always be well **capitalized**. Consequently, every decision should take into account its influence on working capital and fixed costs.

Essentially, you should meet changing consumer needs by being innovative in introducing new or changed products and services. Buyers simply get bored, so alter the packaging and start new advertising campaigns and promotions or product competitions. This should be the norm and not the exception. Remember to continually communicate with your staff, key personnel, directors, partners, and, of course, customers.

Let's look at some additional information that you need to note as an entrepreneur who will continuously require working capital and expansion funds at some point in the future.

Your Business Is Not an Island

At some point, you will need to approach your bank or the higher-risk investors, such as Angel Funds and Venture Capitalists. You will then quickly realize the value of having a well-coordinated business plan. Despite the importance of such a document, many entrepreneurs simply don't have one and will hastily pull one together, using templates found on the Internet.

You must understand that investors get thousands of requests for funding, so why would they choose you? Simply put, you have to impress them to get what you want. This next statement may sound wrong: You need to have a complete understanding of every facet of your business. How is that even possible? If you are hired to run a manufacturing company, should you know how the factory and all its component machinery operate? The simple answer is yes, but in cases of professional CEOs (chief executive officers), the alternative is to ensure that your advisors are knowledgeable about the product and its production.

Having intimate knowledge of the company and all its components (as CEO and as a team) will level the power play between you and professional investors and institutions. This means that you should use a two-pronged approach:

- First, your business plan must highlight that you are the leader and focused on driving the company within the market. This is called a market-driven enterprise.
- Second, you should always be prepared to address the following questions:
  - How much do you require?
  - How will you use these funds?
  - How will you pay these funds back?

A third question has recently come to light, as highlighted in a global aviation project that required $100 million to expand a fleet by 10 aeroplanes. This would add $8 million to profits.

Question: If we invested $150 million in your company, how many aeroplanes could you buy, and how would this influence the bottom line?

The question highlights whether you are prepared for any eventualities. Do you have the systems and spreadsheets in place to enable you to conduct a rapid analysis of the changed circumstances? What they are really asking is whether the added funds will increase the profit ratio due to economies of scale? Will the added funds enable you to gain market share? Or will the added funds place you in a difficult position, as the added aeroplanes may not be filled as demand for goods may not be met?

Sadly, everything you do in a commercial business must be linked to an economic motive. I say "sadly" because as your business expands, you will have to take on more directors and staff and additional capital—so there will be a continual need to interact with more investors. There is always a risk that your focus will change from managing your business to trying to satisfy these investors all the time. My advice is to focus on the business, and the value of the firm will look after itself.

No one can argue with a company that has a solid cash flow, increasing value, strong order books, and growing profits—as well as growing gross profit margins.

Give Investors What They Want

Bottom line: Your ability to communicate with investors is via a business plan. There may be an initial meeting, but it will always end with the investor asking for a business plan and, often, a profile. There is no other way, so prepare one that highlights the passion, skill, experience, and expertise of your team's key managers and directors. It is important when talking to investors to highlight your team's ability to anticipate and manage risk, within a competitive environment. In some instances (depending on the industry), highlight how effective you and your team are in targeting new business markets.

It is quite simple: Give investors what they want—to get what you want. This includes the following:

- Highlight how effective you are in your market and that your business has identified various sources of underexploited market demands.
- Profile your existing business in an easy-to-read four-page document.
- Instead of having a massive document that includes all your research and feasibility studies, have these as separate documents. The profile and executive summaries can refer to specific sections of the industry analysis, research, and forensic audits.
  - At this point, show them an executive summary—the full documents can be made available on request.
- State how much capital you require, how you will use these funds, and a fair and reasonable repayment plan.

Consequently, it is essential to start with the basics to provide a solid foundation for your business. At the outset, you will require a realistic and marketable strategy to secured working capital. The goal is to launch a properly funded business, so you will need initial project funding. A business plan is effectively used as a written proposal to attract capital investment by strategically setting out a blueprint for your planned profitable growth in the short and long term.

Your business plan is effectively more than just a proposal for funding. It is a realistic set of goals and how to achieve them—or, stated differently, a baseline for generating an operating profit before and after financing has been secured.

My intention in this book is to assist you to create a working document that is more than a pretty brochure for investors. It must be a practical tool to guide you and your top management to execute tasks, duties, and responsibilities in a highly professional manner to achieve your company's objectives, profit goals, and mission.

Therefore, take careful note of the following:

- Show indisputable in-depth knowledge of your market and industry in which you intend to operate.

- Show and prove that you have an ability to evaluate how changes in environmental factors (economics, business, politics, and technology) can affect your business.
- Highlight (with examples) your leadership capabilities. In essence, show how you would manage change while maintaining secure operations.
- Highlight your team's skills, experience, and industry depth of knowledge.
- Show that you are experienced and skilled to find market gaps, and show how you would fill such a demand.
- Highlight how you have chosen staff for their skills and experience, but also for their integrity, awareness, intuition, and logic.

I intend to limit long lists of facts as much as possible. In addition, these lists are continuously changing as industries and markets change and, more specifically, when companies have products in various sectors. It is better, therefore, for you to develop your own set of rules to determine for yourself whether your business, concept, or acquisition/merger will be financially viable. These will be developed and explained in later chapters.

Some Thoughts

Running a profitable business is all-encompassing. It takes dedication, dynamic leadership, and never taking your eye off the ball. You have directors and key staff who have duties to complete, but it is still your responsibility to take remedial action when required. Pointing fingers at someone in your firm when something has gone wrong is never the right thing to do. So, without being pedantic, have a paper trail. This can be used later to determine what you did wrong or what you did right under tough circumstances. It effectively becomes a blueprint for the company's future operations.

In today's highly competitive global business environment, you will need to take account of the needs of clients, staff, and directors, and investors' reasons to want to invest in you and your company. A more blunt way of saying this: You must satisfy the myopic greed of people that could make a difference to your company. Before we get into more complexities of business strategy, structure, and so on, the lesson is simple: *Take Total Responsibility*.

Every decision that you make is yours and yours alone. This must become your personal mantra. There is absolutely no other way to operate in the world of business. Always take action only after you have considered the potential repercussions of that action. This is usually conducted by undertaking fair-value analysis and looking at how the business could be affected by your decision. There are those in the market that insist that business is 90 percent gut feel. For them this may be the case, but they also have to admit that their "gut" feel instinct came only after years of losses, successes, and failures and invaluable experience and development of skills.

The following is well worth noting when you run your own business.

- To be effective, a company should always have only one leader.
- Ensure that cash flow always remains strong and within acceptable liquidity ratios.
- Operate in an industry you know, understand, and have passion for and skill to succeed.
- Know who your competitors are and who your potential competitors may be in the future.
- Understand market trends and ensure that your product/services meet current and future demand.
- Know what government and other forms of price regulation in your industry are.
- Control expenses and other liabilities.
- Employ professionals to conduct due diligence, corporate structuring, accounting, forensic audits, legal contracts, and business plans. When you hire experts, don't ignore their advice.
- Have a balanced ratio between work and leisure.

Rainmaker Observation: Set up your strategy document before you launch your business. This will become the blueprint in years to come—not only of how to make a success but also of how to avoid failure.

CHAPTER 2

Knowledge and Survival

Over the years, I have seen so many opportunities lost and watched how some entrepreneurs succeeded in being granted funds, only to kill the funding even before the meeting was over. Many entrepreneurs are poorly prepared when they decide to launch their companies. I need to stress that an inability to take advice from professionals shows an ego that could ultimately ruin your business.

In 2015, I advised a client on how to structure his IT business and wrote a business plan after conducting in-depth research, analysis, and strategy. The entrepreneur stood up and within 7 minutes won the investors over—$20-million funding sealed, but then the ego took over. The investor asked a simple question: "How do you intend to expand your operations in 5 years' time?"

The simple answer would have been to emphasize that expansion within the industry was critical—movement into new territories and so on. Instead, the entrepreneur proudly announced, "Oh, by then I am sure that I will be bored, will have sold my stake, and will have moved on to something else. That is my nature."

This investment loan was repayable over 10 years, but—in an instant—the investors immediately stood up and walked out, not saying a word. The deal had been won and lost within 7 minutes.

In yet another example, an entrepreneur, who prided himself as being an experienced negotiator, was so keen to secure a beneficial deal that he spent way too much time arguing over interest rates proposed by the investors (already 1.5 percentage points below that of other investors), and the opportunity passed him by.

There is no argument that you should try to negotiate the best deal that you can, but how you repay that loan and the interest rates being proposed should only be a consideration of profits lost if you don't get the funding. Simply, if getting funds will enable you to make $10 additional profit per dollar of funding cost, would it make a difference if that profit was $9.5 per funding cost?

Ask yourself: Will the funds enable you to increase profits? Even more pertinent: Do you need these funds?

You are the leader of a company. It is your job to secure the funds and to lead the company and related profit growth into the future. You have directors and managers to ensure that they sweat the new assets, to always get the best results. So before you approach investors, you should have strategized with your team as to what the deal breakers are. For instance, if the funding is payable over too little a time (say 5 years) it may place your company under financial strain.

This book is designed to make you think and to develop your own strategy. There simply isn't a one-size-fits-all strategy that you can download from the Internet. Remember these businesses have directors with different skills and experiences which are influenced by varying geographical areas and types of services offered. If you are the exact copy of another company, how would you survive?

Each chapter of this book aims to provide questions, suggestions, and guides. When you have completed the book, you should be able to have a succinct strategy and business plan, and avoid being a statistic. My 30 years of analysis of companies—from SMEs (small and medium-sized enterprises) to multiglobal conglomerates—have highlighted a simple truth. I believe that failure is a direct result of an inability or lack of desire to undertake proper and effective due diligence, which can then be used to plan for your company's future and then to rigorously pursue your objectives. Remember that a plan does not have to be rigid. Times change and circumstances offer new opportunities, so plans should be flexible enough to take cognizance of potential new trends. Take the opportunity to plan and increase your chances of success. For instance, it is pointless to have a plan that states, "PROFITS MUST INCREASE BY 10 PERCENT A YEAR."

The plan should state how you intend to achieve these profits. If you state that a move to technology will improve productivity and associated ratios, state what your plans are and what the consequences could be.

In fact, if you are inflexible, your chances of being at the forefront of change in business diminish.

It is a truism that being an entrepreneur is never an easy endeavor. Developing a business plan, requesting funding from strangers, and facing the possibility of rejection can be disillusioning and soul destroying.

My personal endeavors in assisting entrepreneurs started in April 2000 after I left stockbroking and set up a consultancy. I quickly discovered hundreds of funding sources who couldn't help me. These funders often weren't interested in companies with long-term goals. As a venture capital company advisor said, "We live in a time of instant millionaires. We are looking to fund companies with that approach." In other words, payback period was nearly always less than 2 years. As I was told, if your business is unable to break even in 18 months, it probably won't.

Shortly thereafter I found that it was easier to take control of the funding process by listing the entrepreneur's company via the numerous methods that stock markets offer around the world. This way, the company raises funding in the form of a sale of its equity and has the added means to return to the market for additional funding in the future. The main issue is that not all companies seek millions of dollars in funding. Some are simply looking for start-up capital or bridging finance. In today's climate, crowdfunding is a very viable option.

Since the year 2000, I have secured important associations with capital providers across the spectrum of markets. My advice is, thus, to conduct your own due diligence as to whom you should approach for funding, or else you could spend valuable time in a multitude of pointless presentations. The ability to conduct a professional presentation to investors is set out in later chapters.

Knowledge Is Survival—Not Just Power

There are a multitude of reasons why entrepreneurs start new businesses, including the freedom from the constraints of the formal work environment, realizing that your earnings are only limited to your skills and not a salary. Yet the realization that financial rewards are not instant and that many months may pass without the security of a monthly salary is a hard lesson for many entrepreneurs. This is particularly tough during the December festive season. My advice is to be very careful when you intend to launch your business. Your plans should include place (city), time, and consideration as to staff, target markets, and so on.

Whatever the reason for setting up your own business, it is a monumental task and will ultimately affect not only you but people you employ and, as a consequence, their families. It is not a responsibility to be taken lightly.

Once you have decided to set up your own company, after considerable thought and self-reflection, accept that being an entrepreneur is a life-changing experience and it isn't for everyone. The position is one where you are your own boss, which also means that you have to take full responsibility for all your actions, both good and bad. It will require determination, an ability to strategize and plan, and a thick skin as media often are less than kind. This includes comprehensive research and analysis of the marketplace and your financial options.

Let me stress again: Successful entrepreneurs know that they have to make difficult decisions every day and that not all will be pleasant.

It thus goes without saying that all businesses start with hope, anticipation, excitement, and goals to change the world of business, but less than 75 percent of all businesses worldwide fail before the end of their first year in operation. This book intends to help you make decisions that will see you survive past these statistics. Being well informed is literally being forewarned against making basic mistakes. *The Rainmaker* will show you some of the elements involved in setting up a business, from the basics of registration to the next phase in becoming established. The aim is thus not to present a comprehensive list of theories and methodologies but to provide brief overviews of areas such as finance, marketing, and creating a strategy and business plan.

For most people, starting a business is indeed an exciting time. The mental image of being mentioned in financial journals, being heralded as a captain of industry is both invigorating and intoxicating, but remember the simple stock market trading axiom: The higher the risk, the higher the reward. Stated differently, the higher the profits you desire, the greater the risk that you will undertake projects that are potentially harmful to the financial security of your business.

It is also a truism that many of the mistakes made by entrepreneurs during the initial start-up phase can be avoided. Some mistakes are linked to rushed decisions and lack of knowledge and experience, but lack of proper implementation of fundamental structures may cost you dearly, such as poorly structured business contracts.

A colleague learnt this lesson the hard way. His contract had a spelling mistake, which meant that—when the company listed on an exchange—he received 2.1 million shares instead of 21 million shares.

It may be obvious to say that you should appoint a lawyer to avoid many of these basic mistakes, but lawyers can be expensive, and you could be led to believe that you can do these yourself. After all, there are many templates on the Internet that can be downloaded for free. However, these templates are designed for general use and do not take your specific requirements into account.

Find a lawyer that may be willing to be a board member and take shares in place of fees. No matter how much research and preparation you do, you will make mistakes when you start a business, but common errors can be avoided, with knowledge and perseverance.

Therefore, an understanding of entrepreneurial basics should provide you with a solid foundation for designing a corporate plan for your company's daily operations and future growth. Companies need capital for start-up fixed costs, daily running operations, and, ultimately, expansion plans. Thus, setting up associations with capital providers should be a valuable lifelong one.

Initially, the goal is to get your company funded. In this case, a business plan is a proposal written to attract capital investment by designing a blueprint for planned profitable growth. Also, your proposal serves as a baseline for generating an operating plan once financing is secured.

Therefore, here are some basic issues that you need to highlight when preparing a winning plan:

- Understand the nature of your market, industry, and business.
- Evaluate the general environment in which your company will operate.
- Set out your company's resources and skills—current and required in the future.

- Your business should target a current market opportunity, which takes advantage of your skills and resources for the improved future structure and growth of your business.
- Set out the skills and experience of key staff and managers/directors.
- Your plan should be driven by market trends and be investor friendly. This means the following:
    - You have identified a niche market that has yet to be exploited.
    - You have conducted scenario plans to generate possible solutions for this expected demand.
    - You have conducted a feasibility analysis of the viability of profits from this business opportunity.

It is interesting that over the years, executives have admitted that some of these guidelines have been useful in preparing effective board-of-directors meeting executive plans, such as seeking approval for new projects or additional cash flow. They confirm that it is critical to always start with a clear description of what it is that you want, show how you will meet your stated corporate goals, and, more importantly, state how your proposal relates to current (researched) market trends and how it will affect profits in the long term.

What Type of Entrepreneur Are You?

When a rainmaker is called in to resolve a problem, often the starting point is to determine what type of entrepreneur you are. Every community within every country has an entrepreneurial culture that has similar traits but with peculiarities to that industry, market, and management styles. These impact the way businessmen and businesswomen think, act, and conduct business. As such, it is the older generation who define the community's entrepreneurial culture, which ultimately impacts on how the younger entrepreneurs act and run their businesses. Identifying traits enables *The Rainmaker* to assist with managerial styles and related problems. Remember that if a rainmaker can identify such trends—or weaknesses—so too can your competitors.

However, an important criterion when trying to understand entrepreneurs is that there is no exact model that defines the entrepreneur.

It will vary from one entrepreneur to another, but no one has yet been able to produce a test that measures and defines a person as having the ability to be an entrepreneur or not. There are also people who exhibit all the criteria that define an entrepreneur but lack entrepreneurial skill.

There are many types and definitions of entrepreneurs as outlined in global research, but experts highlight a range of different descriptions and link them to a scale, as shown in the following figure.

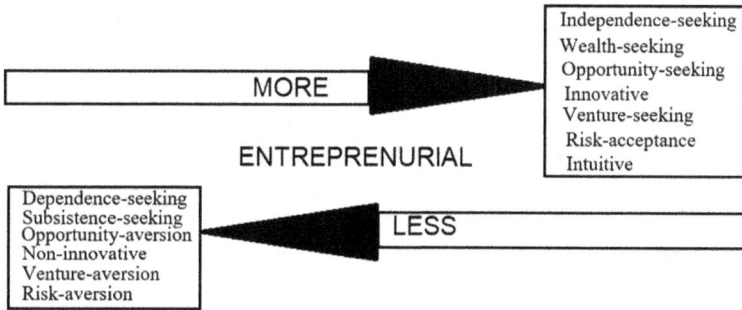

There are always constraints within such models. The key constraint here is that independent laborers, managers, and professionals like lawyers are often not considered entrepreneurs.

For example, the above figure states that an entrepreneur is able to simultaneously be innovative and profit focused, except that innovation tends to be a long-term strategy, which could be opposed by the board of directors, who may have differing levels of acceptance. As such, the entrepreneur will inadvertently start looking for projects that are profitable but may not be innovative, in an effort to seek the board's approval.

As a rainmaker's task is to find where problems are, offer solutions, and then fix problems, the initial task is to always look at the entrepreneur to assess if he or she may be the block to the company's growth. Thus, a good starting point is to understand entrepreneurial traits and characteristics.

Entrepreneurial Groupings

Type	Explanation
Mirroring or copying	• To mirror someone else's strategy and product/services is not sustainable in the long term, as it is uniqueness that differentiates you and your product from your competitors'. They have the advantage of experience and in-depth knowledge of the product and will ultimately get better results than copied products. • The competitors have already spent time, energy, and skill understanding problems, cash-flow constraints, pitfalls, and improved sales techniques. You would be starting out without such experience.
Lifestyle	• A lifestyle entrepreneur is one who builds wealth for personal benefits. • He or she often works longer hours to achieve that personal higher-income lifestyle. • He or she works harder than a high-growth entrepreneur.
High-growth	• A high-growth entrepreneur is focused on wealth creation and rapid growth for the company. • He or she is quite likely to be too risky for the average funding institution, as high growth is often associated with weakened liquidity and solvability ratios.
Ego	• The ego is a defining trait of entrepreneurs and therefore essential to the success of the entrepreneur and his or her company. • However, sadly, many entrepreneurs have massive egos associated with business success. This in turn can lead to overconfidence and, in a worst-case scenario, business failure. • While the ego is an essential driving force, if it is not managed in a beneficial process for the business, it can be a destructive force.

Funders assess entrepreneurs' personalities to ensure that they are self-confident but not overconfident. An overconfident entrepreneur can dramatically increase the risk of business failure and hence increase risks for the funder.

Rainmaker Observation: In today's competitive world, a professional business plan is both a strategy for profit growth and a survival guide against competitors seeking to take market share away from you. At this stage, I have no reason to alarm you, but remember that impediments to profit growth can come from within your company. They are not restricted to competitors. So ensure that a plan accounts for sections that are privy only to directors.

CHAPTER 3

Traits and Successful Directives

Personality Traits of Billionaire Entrepreneurs

I once asked attendees at a book launch, "What is the first thing that entrepreneurs need to do to create a lasting impression?" The answers varied, from having a firm handshake to power dressing. These were so diverse that it became quite obvious that there was no real correct answer but that circumstances would often determine what impressed and what didn't. A young capital provider once arrived at a meeting in shorts and T-shirt. Obviously looked down on, and ignored by other funders, he just didn't seem to care. When it came to signing on the dotted line to provide the funding, these power-dressed executives had a multitude of questions and reasons for wanting to delay providing funding.

The young man stood up and said, "Gentlemen, with my two-penny pen, I would like to sign the $150-million funding required to expand your business." He didn't need expensive clothes, or a branded pen, to impress. He had come to hear the entrepreneur with the intention of investing if he was satisfied that the project was real and met his investment criteria.

So I approached him and asked him the same question I had posed to the book launch attendees.

He answered, "One of the most serious ongoing challenges to entrepreneurs in a roomful of scary people is to maintain honesty and not simply say what people want to hear. That is how you build integrity and honesty among colleagues, staff, and the greater community," adding, "and believe me, it is a very small world."

It is easier to build lasting relationships with people with credibility and trust than it is to assess the truthfulness of those who have a poor pattern of behavior. Even contracts drafted by lawyers have no meaning if trust is an issue.

The following are merely examples of traits that powerful entrepreneurs have displayed over decades. Not all possess these and certainly not all at once, and—more importantly—not all traits are positive.

- **Truth and Credibility:** Never make promises you have no intention of keeping or hope of being able to keep. People around you need to know that what you say is sacrosanct and always linked inextricably to honesty and truth. In effect, keeping promises made or intimated builds trust and solid teams.
- **Egotistic behavior:** Some businessmen and women believe that it is their right to make critical decisions without consulting their fellow board members. Taking unilateral decisions without important input from key partners is arrogant and points to egotistic behavior.
- **An atmosphere of dread:** This style of management may work for a while, but, ultimately, staff turnover increases, with skilled staff poached by friendlier companies. The irony is that many staff will leave for better working conditions and not necessarily higher salaries.
- **Deception:** If you intend to run your company by providing your staff intentionally misleading or incomplete information, it is effectively the same as lying. In the eyes of your staff, you have misled and lied to them.
- **Acceptance of failure:** This is an instant way to gain trust from your staff. When you have made a mistake, admit to it and take responsibility for your actions. While competitors may be rubbing their hands in glee, they will find it increasingly difficult to poach staff. An honest boss engenders loyalty, but failure to simply apologize timely and unconditionally leads to loss of trust.
- **Blaming instead of acting:** In many countries, empowerment or quota systems are enforced, and, whatever your beliefs are, being critical and antagonistic for not getting a promotion, not winning

a tender, or not securing a contract will not earn you favor. In fact, this attitude will hold you back in your career, as such disparagement does ultimately cause suspicion and create permanent resentment toward you.

- **Respect:** The ability to earn respect from competitors is a victory in itself. They may not like you, but if you always act with truthfulness and integrity, you will earn the reputation that you are tough but fair.

- **Shifting blame:** In the early 1950s, there was a trend that if a major problem occurred (e.g., one of your trucks was involved in an accident), the company's specialist team would quickly attend to the matter, not, as you may think, to help the accident victims and thus earn the public's respect, but, instead, to get to the accident scene quickly to paint over the company's logos. This was done to avoid appearing in the newspapers. Shifting the blame does not repair defective components or get stock delivered. Remember, if the company is involved in any way, it is your responsibility to rapidly find a solution.

- **Tough questions:** Too often, I see entrepreneurs avoiding pertinent questions posed by journalists or, even worse, telling outright lies. These are quick ways of destroying your reputation. Rather, think before you answer, and if the question is of a competitively sensitive nature, just say so. People respect honesty, even if they believe you avoided a question.

- **Core values:** When a staff member signs to join your company, or a director accepts a board position, they are effectively saying that they are excited to work with you and are thus placing their trust in your hands. If their trust in you is affected, you will lose their respect. These include affecting their families, quality of life, peace of mind, or their economic security.

- **Mixed signals:** Always ensure that your statements, speeches, or e-mail blasts to staff or customers are not ambiguous. In fact, make sure that whatever you say cannot be misconstrued as such. If you discover that you have made some statements that are ambiguous, take immediate action and clear up any possible misunderstanding.

- **Don't underrate negative influence over staff:** Some entrepreneurs will keep staff guessing as to whether retrenchments will take place. They keep staff guessing—even for months. Instead of giving them the opportunity to find alternative employment, these entrepreneurs adversely affect their lifestyles. The longer this kind of influence takes place, the more likely they are to react emotionally and negatively and then legally.

- **Not being prepared:** A director who believes that there are no questions he cannot answer should be willing to be grilled by an independent panel. When I have listed companies on an exchange, 10 days before the presentation, I set up a panel of experts to hear the director give his presentation. The questions are often brutal but do have the effect of making the presenter realize that he or she does not have all the answers. The system is repeated until the presenter is fully prepared. This system is as effective when presenting to a funding committee or organization.

The preceding examples can become a checklist for being a better leader, who builds trust and credibility with those around him or her. It also serves as a key starting point for analyzing partnerships, associations, and general moral in a company that has inexplicably broken down.

Rainmaker Observation: There is always a reason why trust is affected. It is your choice to decide whether an issue is important or not. However, poor trust in your leader will manifest in staff confusion and, ultimately, negative profit consequences.

CHAPTER 4

Identifying Corporate Mistakes

Having stressed that leaders should have integrity and honesty, let's look at some common mistakes made when businesses begin to show an increase in profits, expand their market share, and move into new products and territories. The issue is that mistakes can cripple a company, but not identifying such mistakes can have a multiplier effect, and then losses tend to increase in intensity.

A truism is that the more time you spend fixing issues, the less time you have to do your designated task, that is, to run your business. We will tackle how to fix issues in later chapters. After dozens of troubleshooting tasks during the past decade, the most common mistake, and arguably the most serious, is a lack of skill in managing a steady cash flow.

Cash Flow Is Always Critical

Simply put, without cash flow, your business comes to a standstill or, worse, crashes. Be diligent in preparing cash flow projections for ongoing operations and extraordinary items such as expansion of assets or movement into new areas. This is textbook theory. I prefer to add an additional factor, which is related to cash flow.

- **A 6-month reserve.** Entrepreneurs tend to underestimate how quickly cash flow can be depleted. You need to have enough cash to pay for daily expenses until your funds from sales flow in. Remember that it may take up to 90 days to get paid for your goods.
- While different industries and markets have varying time frames for payment of invoices, entrepreneurs must plan for inevitable

delays in payments. This is the practical aspect of cash flow, which is seldom highlighted in textbooks. The answer is to be prepared, by developing a realistic business budget to ensure that your cash flow is sustainable for the first 6 months since you launched the business.

- Develop a list of potential expenses and ask bookkeepers, who operate in your industry, whether these are realistic. Bookkeepers are extremely familiar with daily operating expenses, often better equipped than auditors.

Some issues that cause cash flow problems are as follows:

- **Sales are lower than expected.** Your choices are limited without additional funds to carry out additional advertising and marketing. Therefore, your options are to assess why sales are lower than expected and take remedial action or cut costs.
- **Costs increase faster than income generated.** This is often due to productivity falling or input costs rising in response to a change in exchange rates, a hike in interest rates, or increased labor costs. These issues should have been anticipated before the beginning of the financial year. However, there are times when labor strikes cannot be resolved, affecting your source of raw materials. You must have contingency plans in place to offset such eventualities.
- **Split between cash and credit sales.** When you look at ratios, you must split your sales into cash and credit. It is pointless to say that your sales have improved by 80 percent in the past year if your credit sales make up 60 percent of sales and bad debts represent 50 percent of the credit sales.
  - Example: Your sales are $10,000, of which $6,000 is credit. This means that if 50 percent fail to pay, then your actual sales for the year were $7,000.
  - This can place your company under financial strain.
- **Increased Competition.** There is always the possibility that new competitors will enter your market, either directly or via acquisition or investment in the business of an existing competitor. Under such conditions, you have to neutralize competition with better

services and possibly by offering lower prices for the short term. Remember that lowering your prices will impact your cash flow, so a careful analysis as to your break-even point must be carried out.

- **Business cycles.** When your business cycle turns, you need to have cost-cutting plans in place if you don't have other products in a contracyclical business cycle that could offset the downturn.
- **Inefficient sales team not achieving targets.** Have a retrenchment package worked out by your human resources department (internal or outsourced) and implement it when necessary.

Looking at Additional Mistakes

- **A great business will be here tomorrow:** New entrepreneurs need to take a deep breath. Once you have completed market analysis and feasibility studies, you are keen to launch your business. Many textbooks instruct that it is critical to register your business before you start operations.
  - ○ That is true, except that you don't need to incorporate and register your business right away. If you set yourself a target of 3 months to register your business, you will find that you may wish to change the original company name, add new directors to your board, or even change your specific target market.
  - ○ Once your 3 months are up, undertake all the rigorous legal documentation needed to properly launch your business.
- **The difference between ostentatiousness and setting a value tone:** Spending too much on office furniture and decorations will simply impact your cash flow. Your office should look presentable and emulate the market you're in but keep expenses down. You can always upgrade decor when you have reached profit targets.
- **The shotgun approach:** Many entrepreneurs believe that they should control and have a hand in all facets of their business. The strength of successful businessmen and businesswomen is an ability to delegate. This doesn't mean that you lose control of divisions or tasks. Rather, you gain time as you concentrate on your strengths as a leader, and you gain expertise by delegating tasks you are poor at to someone who is better equipped and skilled.

- **Wishful versus realistic goals:** The risk of setting unrealistic and unattainable profit goals creates expectations for staff that may demotivate them when bonuses are not paid on the back of failed targets.
  - ○ Directors usually have profit-share schemes, and if targets are not attained, profit bonuses do not materialize. The essence is to set goals that can be achieved with the resources you have, which must be specific and, more importantly, can be measured within predetermined time frames.
  - ○ Let's not forget that new companies often have investors, who will be more than disappointed that you haven't reached your targets, with some funders demanding their money back, as the norm is to link goals to loan and investment payback time frames.
- **Not taking responsibility:** As leader, it is your obligation to keep your word. Your staff, colleagues, associates, and funders are relying on you. So not researching sales objectives or not reaching the desired market penetration cannot be excused by pointing at competitors or current changing trends or legislation.
- **Strike action or any of a multitude of other possibilities:** Targets are not arbitrary numbers. These should have been derived after analysis of market trends, best-practice feasibilities, supply and demand, strength of the market, product substitutes, and so on. It is critical to carry these out prior to launching a business and you can use strategies such as Porter's Five Forces and PESTEL analysis. Both are discussed in later chapters.
- **Using experts:** While it is always advisable to use experts in critical fields or accounting and law, there is nothing wrong with drafting your own documents and conducting your own research in the initial stages of your company's development. The condition is that you use experts to verify your work. This saves on time-related costs charged by attorneys and auditors.

Ten Fundamental Historic Truisms

It is both a critical and a fundamental reality that launching a new business is a mixture of risk, excitement, and apprehension. The very fact that you are taking the time, effort, and major personal resources boils down to one basic question: *Will my business succeed?*

The essence of this book is to limit the risk of failure but also to answer that very question. The following are 10 of the most important directives to guide you to improve the answer to this basic question.

- **Truism 1: Past performance is not a guarantee of future trends.** Past trends in the industry you are planning to enter will help you to determine value and price of both products and the company. However, only an analysis of future trends based on environmental factors can guide you to choose your products and services. These factors are economics, business, politics, and technology. Each is important to determine whether your company will be successful or not.
    ○ For example, if you are risk averse and do not wish to be involved in a company that buys materials across borders, then stay away from currency-dependent commodities.
- **Truism 2: Your product is just a product.** The aim of your business is to make a profit, so don't be trapped into an emotional attachment with your first product. If it doesn't sell, then change the product. Many businessmen and businesswomen link their reason for starting a business to their first product. Such subjectivity can lead to poor business decisions, which can be harmful to your bottom line.
- **Truism 3: Everyone aims for great.** There are many businesses in the world that are good but only a few that have achieved greatness. As you gain experience and skill, you'll learn to determine how to take your business to the next level. This is discussed in later chapters.
- **Truism 4: The sum of the parts should be greater than the whole.** Once you have launched your business, you need to understand how each part affects the whole. A successful leader learns to talk to his or her staff and build an understanding of the business and its functions from the ground up.
    ○ I once worked for a financial magazine whose editor-in-chief had no clue as to costs and, even worse, how those costs rose drastically if deadlines were not met. It became obvious that he

had no interest in talking to the printers or the drivers who took the magazine copies to the airport. In this example, missing a deadline meant that printers charged overtime, and missing a flight meant that the magazine couldn't be on sale in its destination town. Simply, higher costs together with lower sales are dire for cash flow.

- **Truism 5: Interfering always results in creating more problems.** It is often difficult to relinquish some control of the business to staff you have newly employed. Your task is to run the company, understand how all the parts fit together, and ensure that the status quo is viable and would integrate seamlessly into a bigger and more powerful company in the future.
- **Truism 6: Products and services should be worked hard.** Many companies have assets that are not as productive as they should be. In essence, many businesses possess certain assets that are not exploited. As such, sweating assets means getting the maximum use out of the assets you already possess. You can only really do this if you know how an asset affects other components of the company. Another way of sweating an asset to increase productivity is to use relevant technology.
- **Truism 7: Use available IT.** In order to grow any business, you must take advantage of technology—where can you access the technology, and what are the costs involved?
- **Truism 8: Continually sell your business concept.** Imagine a chance meeting with a highly respected venture capitalist in an elevator. You have maybe 2–3 minutes to "sell" your business concept.
  - There are three simple rules to accomplish this in any situation. First, you must be able to explain what your business does with clarity and ease. Second, to get their attention, you need to display true and honest passion for your business, and, finally, the lasting impression must be one of pride in what your business is achieving.
- **Truism 9: If it's broken—fix it, otherwise don't change anything.** A business that has no problems is a rare one indeed. This does not mean that it is impossible to have a company with no critical issues. So ensure that your company is regularly assessed, changed where required, and realigned for improved productivity.

- **Truism 10: Your time with the company will come to an end.**
  Truly successful businessmen start with the end in mind. They ask
  the question: "What are you starting this business for, and what is
  your aim? At some point, you will want to—or must—retire. Do
  you want to leave a legacy for your family or the business world?
  Do you want to make a difference, or do you just want to retire
  wealthy?"
  - Only you can state what that is. However, having the end in
    mind does set a tone for your business.

Rainmaker Observation: If there was an 11th Rule, it would be *endurance*. Entrepreneurship is not for the faint hearted, what with having to keep up with the multitude of daily demands from staff, clients, and investors and shareholders alike. While you may have employees to handle queries, the final decision will often rest with you, so make sure that you can handle the daily grind both mentally and physically. Issues often ignored in textbooks are nonquantifiable, like handling problems outside your comfort zone, weighing up the opportunity cost of working long hours, and sacrificing family time to attend meetings.

CHAPTER 5

Will Your Business Concept Soar?

I have watched numerous entrepreneurs lose valuable opportunities because they thought the cost of the capital was too high. They spent too much time haggling over the cost of funds while their window of opportunity moved to someone else. Obviously, you always try to attain a good deal, but important factors like the cost of capital should have been discussed prior to investor meetings and investment priorities discussed and agreed to.

Simply, if it costs you one dollar to make two dollars, are you winning or losing?

Bookstores and online e-commerce gateways are full of financial self-help books, from pure academic to highly personalized trading books. These books will assist you to understand corporate structures, financing methods, strategy, and business planning. While *The Rainmaker* will allude to such issues, the focus is on what structures are most conducive to making a success of your business, followed by techniques to keep the business healthy and prepared for future growth.

The following are some of the pertinent issues *The Rainmaker* questions:

- How prepared are you and your business? For leadership, growth, accessing capital, and the rigorous and tough daily decisions you will have to face and make?
- How have you structured your business? Did you take into consideration corporate guidelines and government-to-local legislation?

- Do you have a documented and workable strategy and business plan? Can you adapt this to a powerful presentation to capital providers?
- Do you have a strong presentation for directors, key managers, staff, and capital providers?

This book is designed to be practical, while taking theory into consideration. Global statistics show that between 75 percent and 90 percent of all new businesses fail within 2 years of being launched. I believe that there is a direct link between failure and the lack of establishing a workable strategy and to carry out that strategy in a coordinated manner. The solution seems so simple: Take the opportunity to carefully plan your future to raise the chances of profit and ultimately success.

My involvement in funding businesses accelerated in 2010, when I helped raise $20 million and $150 million in two extremely different projects. The first project was to acquire a mine in Kenya, and the second was to acquire and launch a new aviation charter company in South Africa. It took less than 8 minutes to raise the funds for the purchase of the mine. The entrepreneur started his presentation, but the funder simply raised his hand and said, "I have read the business plan and supporting documents. Based on these, we agree to the proposed deal."

The second project presentation, this time to a Chinese consortium, took place in Bangkok. That presentation took three 1-hour sessions over 3 days. On the fourth day, photographers were at the meeting to document the deal. Hands were shaken, and the transfer of funds was carried out as discussed.

These two projects did, however, give me a skewed perception of how really difficult funding truly is. The next dozen projects were not so easy, with entrepreneurs fumbling presentations, shortcuts taken by researchers, and the financials proving to be padded to increase bottom-line growth.

Many projects were not funded, and I had to take a step back to reassess my methodology. Over the following years, I developed a system that included research to support forecasts on audited financials and corporate structures that met the latest legislative guidelines and regulations.

The system worked well until 2015, when I had to reassess and develop new methodologies, as outlined here:

Two Contradictory Methods

Formal Analysis

There is nothing worse than being asked a question by an investor that you don't know the answer to. So to reduce the failure of not attaining capital raising, the following three essential nonnegotiable phases to successful rainmaking may be considered:

1. **Due Diligence.** In other words, take the company apart. Conduct due diligence on every aspect of the firm, including checking the basics, such as whether the company is registered, has and owns patents and trademarks, owns factories or warehouses, and so on. You must view these assets yourself. An investor once asked me whether I had visited the production plant, which was in another country, and, given the time frame to complete the documentation, I had not visited the company's premises.
    a. Essentially, the following must be assessed:
        i. **Financials:** Ensure that the financials are up to date. Then conduct analysis and forecasts, formulate a valuation, and undertake ratio analysis.
        ii. **Corporate structure:** (including the board of directors) and whether they meet international corporate governance and transparency criteria.
        iii. Ensure that your feasibility study is clear and concise. If the report is lengthy, draft a four-page executive summary.
2. **Research and feasibility.** This enables you to find out whether the company meets international best-practice trends and whether forecasts are within industry ranges.
    a. This includes PESTEL analysis, Porter's Five Forces, SWOT analysis, and legislation related to funding, listing, and government-specific legislation.
3. **Strategy workshops.** To ensure that all the preceding requirements have been assessed and understood, a series of workshops should be conducted with the entrepreneurs. It is at this stage that corporate structure can be corrected and financials adjusted to meet International Financial Reporting Standards (IFRS) compliance regulations.

a. Make sure that there is consensus in a direct and clear decision to proposed changes.

b. Appoint a team, preferably a driven and reliable one, to ensure that an action list is carried out.

c. The appointed team should monitor changes with effective communication structures and report back schedules to update management as to the progress of the project.

Next, it is time to write the relevant documents. This may include a business plan (ensure that this meets the exchange listing requirements), a prospectus, and a strategy for the group. The latter document is different from the business plan as it contains specific tasks and goals for directors and key staff.

The Creative Approach

Some economists say that this method is not really in opposition to the more formal analytical method of analysis of your company. In fact, it is often the lack of creativity that leads companies into the financial abyss. *The Rainmaker* usually starts here, looking at how you conduct your business before assessing the more factual statistics. Indeed, everyone has those facts, but not all entrepreneurs have the ability to run a company and solve issues that could impede new paths of profitability with creative thinking.

Defining Creativity

This implies the ability of an entrepreneur to generate new ideas and approaches to company strategy and management. Stated from an economic perspective, this involves the ability to identify opportunities based on these new ideas and approaches and to turn them into economically viable products and services.

Environmental aspects that may influence creativity can be broken down into four factors, namely, economics, business, politics, and technology, including the availability of resources such as capital, people, expertise, skills, competition, Socio-economic conditions, and government and business regulations and guidelines.

It is interesting to note that even when creative flair is present, there is no guarantee that creativity will occur. So whichever method you deem perfect for you, the true entrepreneur leaves no stone unturned to turn vision into action. In combining the two methods, creativity becomes an analytical process whereby the current task is strategized to achieve a path to your desired financial outcome.

It must also be noted that many companies see a creative process solely as an expense.

Starter Questions

Before we delve into the necessary basics, I have a short list of questions that you should regard with brutal honesty. This chapter has asked whether your concept has what it takes to fly and succeed. Actually, the question should be whether you have the ability to steer the company to success. The following list requires a simple *yes* or *no* answer. If you get more *no* than *yes* answers, it's time to look at some harsh realities. Maybe you don't have what it takes to start and run your own business.

Every new entrepreneur should consider the following 10 questions:

Question	YES	NO
1. Are you calm when all hell breaks loose around you?		
2. Do you take responsibility for your decisions and actions?		
3. Are you a natural leader?		
4. How well do you handle pressure?		
5. How well do you communicate?		
6. Are you a fair and just person?		
7. Are you able to admit when you need help and then employ required skills?		
8. Do you have the endurance needed to be successful?		
9. Are you able to make tough decisions?		
10. Do you inspire people to follow you?		

Rainmaker Observation: The role of *The Rainmaker* is to help you make things happen, from structuring your business to being profitable to raising capital. There is a dire need worldwide for SMEs to succeed; thus, writing this book should make the process of achieving your financial goals easier, while assisting in employment creation.

CHAPTER 6

Necessary Basics

The Rainmaker is written to help current and prospective businesses to increase their potential to become profitable in the global market. Once a profitable status has been attained, productivity and efficiency must be raised before expansion is undertaken.

My primary goal is thus to present a way of thinking that will help you plan, launch, and successfully operate your business. Shortcuts are never recommended and should not even be considered.

You should always be in a position to evaluate various business decisions yourself, so that if you decide to pursue an idea or market opportunity, you can then develop a thorough feasibility and business plan. Preliminary work should put you well ahead of your competitors with an effective structure for your business.

Entrepreneurship Defined

The concept of entrepreneurship was first established in the 1700s, and the meaning of the word "entrepreneur" has evolved today into a more complex term than simply meaning someone who runs a business. To some economists, an entrepreneur is a person willing to bear the risk of starting a new venture after having assessed the possibility of making a profit—whether the project be a short- or a long-term one.

Another definition states that entrepreneurs are people who are willing to develop new goods or processes that they have identified as what the market needs but are not currently being supplied. Regardless of the definition, experts across the globe accept the undeniable truth that entrepreneurship is the leading activator stimulating economic growth and employment opportunities in all spheres of society. In emerging nations, successful small businesses are the main driving forces of job creation, income growth, and massive poverty alleviation. Therefore, government and private support for entrepreneurship is crucial for the well-being of any society. More importantly, entrepreneurship empowers people to change current thinking and innovate for the future.

The current trend is toward knowledge-based economies, which will increasingly impact on how entrepreneurs conduct business. Essentially, the many complex functions and regulations required to run a successful enterprise have resulted in many companies outsourcing specific functions to consultants, who still do the same work for the company but carry out these functions from their own offices.

What are the implications of this setting? How will these factors influence your business? Will the cost of outsourcing increase or decrease your market share? Is your product or service globally marketable if consultants are in control of such decisions? If so, who are your competitors now?

Basic Business Principles

The more difficult and complex the global world of business becomes, the more intricate the entrepreneur's corporate structures, in turn, become. While there are many sound and focused business principles, which entrepreneurs may successfully follow, the next 10 principles form the basis of sound and ethical business practices.

Step 1: Top 10 Business Theories

1. Never lose focus on what your core product or service is.
2. Continually assess what your target market is and whether this has changed.
3. Ask yourself what your competitive strength is.
4. Set realistic corporate goals and objectives.
5. Ensure that you have (and adhere to) strict cash flow management policies.
6. Manage employees, key personnel, and directors.
7. Manage stakeholder expectations.
8. Continually market and promote your business.
9. Be innovative, especially through tough economic times.
10. Always be ethical.

The question is, however, how to establish a set of guidelines to determine answers to the foregoing business principles. What must an entrepreneur analyze to achieve a viable and ultimately profitable set of entrepreneurial operational guidelines?

While there are a variety of corporate models that entrepreneurs can follow, there are some basic principles that form standard operating principles around the world. They are represented here in the form of a step-by-step guide for entrepreneurs to follow before launching their enterprises.

Step 2: Pre-start-up To-Do List

Steps	Phase	Questions
1	Information	The following questions must be answered at the outset to determine the core product to be targeted. • Identify a market opportunity. • Determine how this demand can be met. • Assess various business models available to achieve the above. • What is the target market? • Who will be the funders? • What is the business environment?
2	Get organized	Once a target market has been identified, assess the following: • Who will run the business? • Who will assist and in what capacity? • Where will your business be situated? • What is your communication strategy? • What legal form should your business take?
3	Feasibility study	To identify a target market efficiently, a feasibility study needs to be conducted, including the following: • Demographics • Competition • Start-up and operating costs • What sites are available and suitable, at what cost? • Feasibility can also be subdivided into macroenvironmental, social, financial, legal, and business.
4	Review findings	• Results from the feasibility study are assessed, and a decision on whether to proceed or abandon the project is made. When feasibility is neither positive nor negative, the entrepreneur needs to reassess the project and its viability.

Steps	Phase	Questions
5	Funders	• Determine how many employees you will require and the related costs. • Draft a profile and a business plan to attract potential investors. • The profile should contain information about management, product, and expected return on investment. • Set up solid and transparent record-keeping systems.
6	Planning and financing	• This step involves the use of the above information to finalize a business plan. Remember to refer to the feasibility report throughout the plan. • The business plan must include financial forecasts and how these are to be achieved and backed by research.
7	Begin operations	Once financing has been secured, the entrepreneur still has to decide whether the project should be launched. • Set up management structures. • Appoint project leaders. • Acquire the necessary equipment. • Develop operating policies.

In summary, the preceding outline simply states that as a precursor to investing time and money in a new project, a macroenvironmental audit must be undertaken to scrutinize broad issues over which your company has no or little control. Ask: *How would political, social, economic, and demographic factors such as the exchange rate, affirmative action, crime, and human resources affect your business?*

A macroaudit is usually a three-part research and analysis process that includes Porter's Five Forces analysis, PESTEL analysis, and SWOT analysis. These are set out in later chapters.

Step 3: Is There a Market Opportunity?

- Is your proposed business based on a thoroughly assessed opportunity in the marketplace?
- Is your idea a response to personally identified need(s) in the marketplace that you found had not been met? Ask specific questions:
  ○ What research and analysis have you conducted to confirm that the demand really exists?

○ Is this opportunity available now, in both the short and the long term? The question really looks at the viability of this project over time (e.g., what is the ratio of costs to potential profits?)

○ Could this business idea lead to additional market opportunities in future? If you believe that it could, conduct further research on global and regional trends to identify what these opportunities may be.

Step 4: Do You Plan to Exploit a Niche Market?

• Start with an analysis of potential customers in that new target market.

  ○ How do you plan to research and get information about these potential customers?

    ▪ Are these customers similar or the same as those whom you are already targeting?

    ▪ If so, will you be selling new services directly to these customers?

      ‣ If not, what will your marketing strategy be?

      ‣ Do you aim to target on-sellers, such as distribution companies or wholesalers?

    ▪ Once the preceding issues have been assessed and resolved, undertake the following:

      ‣ Categorize these potential customers into groups and describe your marketing strategy.

      ‣ What market distribution channels will you use to reach these different groups of customers? Will these include cold calling, mailshots, and general broader advertising and promotional campaigns?

      ‣ Have you calculated the industry's market size and value?

        ▷ How did you calculate the market size, in number of customers and in value?

      ‣ What is your market penetration strategy?

Step 5: Are There Substitutes for Your Idea?

- Now brainstorm what potential risks there may be to launch your new product.
- Assess potential alternatives to your planned strategy. Are there better products on the market? Are there cheaper products on the market? Should you rethink your strategy?
- Review your list of alternatives and select the best strategy to respond to customers' demands.
- Answer the following questions for each of your business ideas:

Issues	Questions
Competition	• Is your concept unique? • What makes it unique? • Can your concept be copied? • Can you get the product to market before competitors do? • What is the time frame before competition sets in?
Time frames	• How much time is needed for the pre-start-up phase of this business? • How long is your window of opportunity? • What milestones must be achieved before you launch this product? Can the time frames be shortened? • What are the business, market, and industry risks associated with the product?
Risk	• Has anyone tried this or a similar concept before? • What were their results? • How long did it take for them to get started? • What can you learn from their experience?
Other considerations	• What other macroeconomic variables could affect the launch and running of the product?

Step 6: Market Analysis and Research

Many businesses will require some external research to accurately forecast demand for products or services. There are two basic methods to obtain such data:

Secondary Data:

- Public and Internet libraries.
- Available market studies and industry information, especially from the major accounting houses.

- Analysis of listed companies in similar sectors.
- Market, industry, and economic forecasts.
- Trade unions and industry associations.
- Electronic search engines, with specific focus on doctoral theses.

Primary Data:

- Talking to people in the industry.
- Observing and interviewing similar businesses.
- Suppliers, vendors, and bankers.
- Conducting market surveys.

Step 7: The Five Stages of Business Life Cycles

The life cycle of any organization affects economies as companies grow, mature, and then decline. To sustain the life of any business, you will need to innovate and continually improve your efficiency and production and the time it takes you to get your product to market. Adding new products and services that are contracyclical to your current offering should always be considered.

This is an ongoing process. The following is a basic overview of business cycles, namely, launch, growth, shake-out, maturity, and decline:

Stage 1: Launching the Company Or New Products or Services

Notable trends during this phase are as follows:

- Your company's sales are low as you enter new markets.
- Your revenue is low, and initial start-up costs are high.
- Businesses are prone to incur losses in this phase. The norm is to achieve breakeven after 18 months.
- In fact, throughout the entire business life cycle, profits lag behind the sales cycle and create a time lag between sales growth and profit growth.
- Cash flow during this phase is under strain owing to start-up costs and additional capitalization.

Stage 2: Uptrend or Growth

Notable trends during this phase are as follows:

- As sales increase, businesses start seeing profit once they pass the break-even point.
- However, as the profit cycle still lags the sales cycle, the profit level is not as high as sales.
- Assuming that there are no extraneous and unexpected expenses, cash flow during the growth phase should become positive.

Stage 3: Shake-Out

Notable trends during this phase are as follows:

- This phase is really the start of the maturity phase.
- Sales growth starts to slow.
- This is due mainly to market saturation or new competitors entering the market.
- Focus shifts toward expense reduction, and consolidation starts.
- Sales peak during the shake-out phase.
- Profits start to slow during this phase.
- This slower growth in sales and decline in profit cause a strain on cash flow.

Stage 4: Flattening of the Cycle or Maturity

Notable trends during this phase are as follows:

- Sales decrease.
- Profit margins get weaker.
- Cash flow remains virtually unchanged.

As firms approach maturity, capital spending should have been completed, and cash flow should be higher than the profit stated on the income statement.

It is important to note that many businesses extend this phase by introducing new products or technologies to further the growth of existing products and services.

Stage 5: Down Cycle or Decline

Notable trends during this phase are as follows:

- Sales, cash flow, and profits decline.
- Companies that haven't managed the process via the introduction of new products or technologies during the shake-out phase tend to lose competitive edge.

Rainmaker Observation: *The Rainmaker* is often called in during the maturity or decline phases to assess why product sales and hence profits have declined. The assessment is simple: No entrepreneurial activity during these stages of a life cycle equals lost market share, which often cannot be regained.

CHAPTER 7

Essential Legal To-Do List

Choosing a Company Name

Choosing a name for your company may seem an easy task, but note that it becomes an integral part of the company's identity and therefore should portray your intentions to, among others, customers, staff, and investors. For instance, it would make no sense to call a financial services company "Fish and Chips Ltd."

Consider the following:

- The company name that you choose must be different from that of companies who have already legally registered. This includes the use of signs and symbols.
- Offensive words in a company name will always be disallowed.
- Names that suggest an association to legal bodies or government links will not be accepted.
- Your company name should be linked to the product or service that you are offering.
- Your company name should be easy to pronounce and remember.
- Having a location in a name could limit future growth or confuse buyers.

Choosing an Address

- A registered office address is the official address of the company where all legal, contractual, and statutory mail will be sent to.
- The address should appear on your letterhead, business cards, and e-mails.
- Remember that the public have access to these details, so it is preferred that you separate your personal contacts, address, and e-mails from your business.

Location and Pricing

Here are some guidelines.

Issues	Note
Location	Your office should never be located in any of the following: • A basement. • A cul-de-sac. **Assess the following:** • Who your other tenants are. This could impact your business directly or indirectly. • Whether higher rents indicate high foot traffic. • Whether your clients or customers would be comfortable coming to your office. • Whether there is enough parking for clients, customers, funders, etc.
Pricing	**Note:** • Never compete on price; everyone loses in a price war. • Instead of using price to attract customers, offer extra services to entice customers. • Be different from your competitors. • Gauge the difference between markup percentage and gross profit margin percentage. These will influence your ability to manage price and discount strategies and still make a profit.

Licenses, Insurance, and Taxes

The types of licenses that you will require will depend on the legal structure that you choose for your business, which includes sole proprietorship, corporation, partnership, or limited liability company.

- Obtain the proper licenses that apply to your choice of business structure.
- Approach insurance and assurance companies, and get quotes for worker compensation, keyman insurance, and property and movable assets protection.
- If your company has a unique logo, it is recommended that you apply for a trademark.
- Appoint qualified lawyers, bookkeepers, and tax experts.
- Different countries have various value-added tax (VAT) legislation, so obtain the correct limits and obligations. Remember that the VAT records that you keep must be detailed and include all business transactions, bills, and receipts.

Forms of Enterprises

- Many countries have different forms of corporate structures, so I have outlined those that are common around the world. These are formally regulated and governed by the respective countries' varying companies acts, and relate to how a new company can be formed, how such a company conducts business, and when a company can be liquidated.
- Companies may be either private or public, as set out in the following table.

Type	Details
Nonprofit	• Formerly called *Section 21 Companies*, this form is established to be of benefit to the general public, such as religious or charity-type organizations. • All income and assets can only be used for the promotion of the organization's nonprofit objectives.
Profit	• Public company: the name ends in "Ltd." • Private company: the name ends in "Pty Ltd." • Personal liability company: the name ends in "Inc." • Partnership. • Business trust. • Sole proprietorship. • External company (branch of a foreign company).

The most used corporate structure is the private company, as it is one that is perceived to have serious legal structures for the long term. It is, in fact, the correct structure for most entrepreneurs who wish both to have a legal entity that holds all business risk and to be taken seriously.

Directors, Shareholders, and Other Details

To set up a limited company, you will need to be able to provide information on the following:

- **Directors' details:** Generally, most countries will state that you must have at least one registered director, who is at least 16 years old and who cannot have been declared bankrupt or banned from being a company director.

- ○ You will need the following information:
  - ■ Their full names.
  - ■ Date of birth.
  - ■ Nationality.
  - ■ Occupation.
  - ■ Country of residence and residential address.
  - ■ Note that some countries permit a company to act as a director.
- **Shareholders' details:** The norm is that there should be at least one shareholder. While some shareholders are also directors, this is not always a requirement.
  - ○ You will need the following information:
    - ■ Their full names.
    - ■ Residential address.
    - ■ Number of shares and value per share.
  - ○ Shareholders are entitled to the following:
    - ■ Dividends, if paid.
    - ■ To vote at annual general meetings.
- **Key personnel and stakeholders:** They can include investors, employees, customers, and suppliers. In recent years, stakeholders have been expanded to include communities, government, and trade unions.
- **Customers:** They are simply defined as individuals, groups of people, or organizations that buy goods or services from you. As customers are generally influenced by price and quality, an entrepreneur should always take these variables into consideration prior to launching any new product or service.
- **Suppliers**: Also called vendors, they are universally defined as anyone who supplies goods or services. However, suppliers must be distinguished from contractors or subcontractors, who sell a value-added service or product.
  - ○ Significance of suppliers:
    - ■ Entrepreneurs, together with key staff, must make critical decisions when buying raw materials. A wrong decision could significantly impact profits, so suppliers are selected based on price, quality, and what added services they offer.

- While price is often a major consideration, always look at the relationship that you may have with the supplier. This is as important as price. If a crisis happens, the business may be able to call for assistance from its supplier.
- **Business identity:** In ensuring that a company has a reputable identity, entrepreneurs need to check that *corporate social responsibility* and its following three basic disciplines are in place:
  - ○ **Compliance** to ensure that they currently have complied and will comply in the future with all necessary corporate regulatory requirements and legislation.
  - ○ **Reputation enhancement** to always deliver on its promises to all stakeholders to uphold its reputation as being efficient and professional.
  - ○ **Value add** refers to the additional services that a supplier offers. These features provide entrepreneurs with a competitive edge over other companies with otherwise more expensive products.

The Rainmaker tends to look at the inner circle of the entrepreneur, the financial director, and key shareholders as an indicator of the competence of the company to achieve sound profits. However, global stockbroking corporate advisors are increasingly assessing the outer circle to determine how the environment will influence management in their decisions related to products and services.

Compliance Is Not Pandering

Businesses are not expected to pander to staff.

At times, *The Rainmaker* is called into a company to resolve staff disputes. This is not the task of *The Rainmaker*, but what can be said is that entrepreneurs must find a balance between staff, directors, and managers and the realities of the business itself. This means considering issues that affect both staff and the business. There should be strategies in place to hire the correct staff and plans to deal with dissatisfaction among staff.

Rainmaker Observation: There needs to be both pre- and after-sales strategies. Clients should be happy to buy the product and even happier to recommend it to friends and families.

CHAPTER 8

Developing Priorities

In a world where opportunity costs must constantly be taken into account, entrepreneurs walk a tightrope between making correct and effective decisions, which can either win or at times fail. A decision that worked for a situation may not work for the same situation again.

Why is that?

The simple answer is that the circumstances of a situation do not remain the same at all times. There will always be something different, such as political events or elections, volatile exchange rates, economic release of statistical data, and a host of other possible macroeconomic variables. There is a dire need to understand that each decision must be made on a sound foundation of knowledge, as pertaining to that specific time and place. Experienced entrepreneurs (and investors) know the value of the following essentials when approaching an issue (on which a decision must be made):

- Knowing the organizational structure of the company (involving directors, management, and key staff).
- Using latest financial models and ratios.
- Devising an effective advertising and marketing plan.
- Analyzing thoroughly the quality and price of product or services.

Vision, Mission, and Goals

The vision, mission, and goals should assist the entrepreneur to hone down the targets to be achieved into manageable sections.

Assume a corporate strategy for 5 years:

- The vision would be of a 5-year view.
- The mission would be of a 3-year view.
- The goals would be of a 1-year view.

It is a broad view of what must be achieved within those timelines in order to accomplish corporate and business strategies. However, these timelines can be flexible depending on how rapid the company grows, how quickly targets are met, and how profit has been achieved.

Setting Goals

Having your short- and long-term goals written down is a strong attribute of powerful entrepreneurs.

Milestones	These are critical stages in the development of the company. These objectives are broad but do assist in providing directors with direction to achieve priorities.
Short-term	This tends to mean a 1-year plan to achieve more specific goals. These defined goals also help to highlight to investors how you are achieving your pro-forma income within the parameters set out in the short-term goals.
Long-term	You can't expect anyone (investors, directors, and staff) to believe you with a long-term strategy if you haven't achieved the short-term goals. If you have achieved the short-term goals, however, keep the long-term strategy and goals realistic.
Exit strategy	Funders all want to know how and when you plan to repay the funds invested in your company. They will ask you whether your company will generate enough cash flow to cover the debt, whether you intend to list on a stock exchange, and so on. Knowing what these questions may be should assist you to be better prepared to raise funds.
Family, business associates, and directors	As a director and a shareholder, you will be spending a lot of time at work. It is prudent to make sure that people know and accept this. It is simply better to ask what they expect from you than trying to guess what will be acceptable or not. Take the time to find out what your business associates expect of you and communicate what you expect from them.

Making a Profit

The growth of your business is dependent on profits while managing cash flow. Without profit, cash flows will fall, and without cash flow you cannot acquire the materials that you need to make a profit.

To increase profits, you can do the following:

- **Increase the price of the products or services that you are selling.** It is important not to increase your prices so high as to drive potential customers away to your cheaper competitors, but a small increase in price can lead your product or service being perceived as being more valuable.

- **Decrease your costs**.
  - ○ **Variable costs:** These are the costs incurred in producing or buying the products.
    - ▪ Decreasing variable costs is possible if you can negotiate better deals with suppliers or implement logistics and technology to decrease the time it takes you to get your product to market.
  - ○ **Fixed costs:** These are the costs incurred regardless of how much you sell, for instance, the cost of electricity needed to run your factories.
    - ▪ Fixed costs can be reduced in various ways but requires productivity and cost management expertise. You could make the wrong decision in your endeavor to save costs.

Competition

Know your competition. You can bet that they know you, your pricing strategies, quantities you are selling, and your target markets.

Complementary Products

Show that you have researched all companies that offer competitive or related products to yours. Define those who offer complementary services in the same industry or similar industries. Assess whether you should tackle competitors head on or negotiate possible joint ventures, strategic partnerships, buyouts, acquisitions, etc.

Assess at least three of your strongest major competitors. Research them in terms of market share, their directors' years in business, experience, and skill. Then assess price strategy, products or services sold, and their advantages and disadvantages in the market, compared to your company and services.

As such, compare your strengths and weaknesses to your competition's and consider factors like location, resources, reputation, services, and personnel. It is also vital that you demonstrate an expert understanding of what your industry is all about, from a historical account to future best-practice trends.

Here are some basic questions:

- Why are current market distribution channels the way they are?
- Can these channels be improved on?
- How did your competitors achieve their market share?
- What advertising, marketing, and promotional strategies did your competitors use effectively to achieve sales goals?

Establishing a Mission

The tone and meaning of your mission statement should explain why you started the business.

Therefore, a mission statement is a short summary of your business' purpose, what its goals are, the kind of product or service that you aim to provide to primary customers and market, and where it intends to conduct such operations.

Analyze Your SWOT

These are your business strengths, weaknesses, opportunities, and threats. Be thorough to the point of being brutal, and your analysis should help you to draft a better strategy and a plan based on critical and unemotional points of reference.

Once you have completed this task, conduct a SWOT analysis on the industry and then assess how you fare relative to the rest of the industry.

Develop a Plan

SWOT helps you develop strategies to take advantage of your strengths in the marketplace, make changes to correct weaknesses, take the opportunities to expand into new markets, and draft strategies to tackle your threats.

Remember to distribute tasks among key managers, which helps to nullify an atmosphere of negativity.

Create a Budget

A budget helps you to identify specific expenses that can be reduced and effectively helps you to make financially sound strategic decisions.

Make It a Living Document

Whether you have drafted a strategy, a list of goals, or a business plan, make it a living document accessible to your staff. Remember to make your plan look like a "to-do list," which is delegated and communicated to directors and key staff.

Your plan should be challenging, achievable, and regularly reviewed.

Pull It Together

This aim here is to give you a systematic building block approach to successful entrepreneurship to place you in a position that ensures the following:

- That there is order instead of chaos in your thinking and implementation.
- That efficiency improves because of properly executed decisions.
- That opportunity for success is improved.

The preparation of a credible document, whether a proposal or a strategy, always requires time and input from relevant parties, management, and key staff. The steps from effective documentation to implementation are set out in the following schematic:

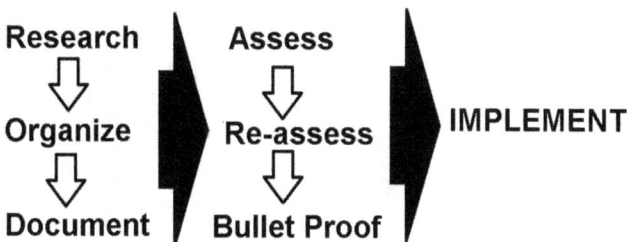

Research ⇩ Organize ⇩ Document → Assess ⇧ Re-assess ⇩ Bullet Proof → IMPLEMENT

Rainmaker Observation: Remember that the goal is to prepare documents that are strategic in nature for first your business and second for investors, potential new partners, and directors. As such, any plan must be succinct and written in a knowledgeable, compelling, and effective manner.

CHAPTER 9

Evaluation of a Business Concept

In this chapter we will look at new concepts and ideas, assess viability, and highlight the following:

- The critical need for a thorough evaluation of any business idea prior to implementation.
- Analysis of the viability of using technology for this new idea.
- Selecting a product or service.
- The supply–demand model.

However, as boring as it may seem and as time-consuming as it appears to be, all new business ideas, no matter how brilliant you may appear to be, must be assessed in a feasibility study to truly determine its effectiveness in the real world. As such, this chapter highlights whether your business idea can survive and prosper as a stand-alone entity within your larger organization, to become marketable and ultimately profitable. The next chapter assesses ideas through more analytical feasibilities.

Evaluating Business Ideas

Unfortunately, the truth is that not all business ideas are good, viable, or even profitable.

Many entrepreneurs know that they are risking all their private assets and reputation when they start their own businesses. While a feasibility study will not eliminate failure, it does increase the odds of success based on improved knowledge into the market, the industry, and how your specific idea fits within these variables. You will then effectively be able to make an informed decision as to what you are letting themselves in for and the likelihood of it succeeding.

Prior to discussing the feasibility studies, general pitfalls that may occur when selecting a business opportunity are discussed.

Opportunities and Pitfalls

Businesses fail for many reasons, and not all are technical or cash flow related. Inadequate turnover might be caused from economic conditions beyond your control. While declining sales could be a direct result of poor corporate and/or business strategy, it could also be owing to changing economic cycles or environmental factors such as terror attacks, natural disasters, or global political disruptions.

The most common reasons for small business failure include the following:

- Management or key staff incompetence.
- Egoism.
- Inadequate start-up capital.
- Low barriers of entry and thus too many competitors.
- Ineffectual advertising and promotion campaigns.
- Lack of cash-flow management.
- Ignoring changing market and industry trends.
- Little or no competitive edge.
- Poorly located business premises.
- Poor financial management control.
- External factors, such as economic conditions and changes in legislation.

This incompetence is often really a lack of proper training and inexperience about what constitutes effective marketing, promotional, financial, and production techniques. Consequently, *The Rainmaker* assesses whether you have fallen into age-old pitfalls, as follows:

- Are you subjective as to the efficacy of your business, idea, or project?
- Have you undertaken thorough market research to ensure that supply and demand weighs in your favor?

- Have you checked that your product or service will meet quality standards?
- Have you checked that your financial forecasts or budgets are realistic and are based on latest statistics and trends?
- Have you double-checked that sales forecasts are not too optimistic?
- Have you checked your competitors' products or services to ensure that your offering is sufficiently different to make it unique?
- Do you understand all legal requirements to run your business, from a legislative, government, and corporate point of view?
- Have you appointed experts to review your strategies?
- Have you employed a team that is skilled and experienced in your selected business environment?
- Do you understand the life cycle of your product?

The aim of a feasibility study or due diligence is to assist you to identify potential problems (before they occur) for your new business or potential new product and help to find solutions to these problems.

If you are diligent in the foregoing aspects, investors will gain an incredible insight into your approach to running a business. You will have answered their critical questions before the interview even starts: Is this entrepreneur diligent, does he or she know what is going on in his or her business, does he or she pay attention to detail, is he or she serious about business, and does he or she have the necessary skills and experience to run the company successfully?

What Is Your Business Idea?

Prior to conducting an expensive feasibility study assess your idea along broader trends. You should still note these findings in a formal document, which usually forms the first step in the more in-depth feasibility studies. Here, as a starting point, we look at possibilities, socioeconomic and business conditions, and the potential profit outcome of your planned idea.

This method is important because it places management decisions on record, as these decisions could have a major impact on the company if major corporate deals are carried out, such as the purchase of a company, merger, listing the company, or moving into new markets.

Choosing Products and Services

Selecting a product or a service that is expected to be in demand in the near future is key to the success of the business as this forms part of strategy and, in particular, your business model or plan. When reviewing pricing, always remember that high-volume goods are often linked to lower profit margins. The profit as a percentage and as a dollar value on bread is much lower than on Mercedes cars. Bread is a volume-based business, and this must be reflected in the margins and the volumes.

This is best illustrated with the following diagram:

Supply–Demand Model

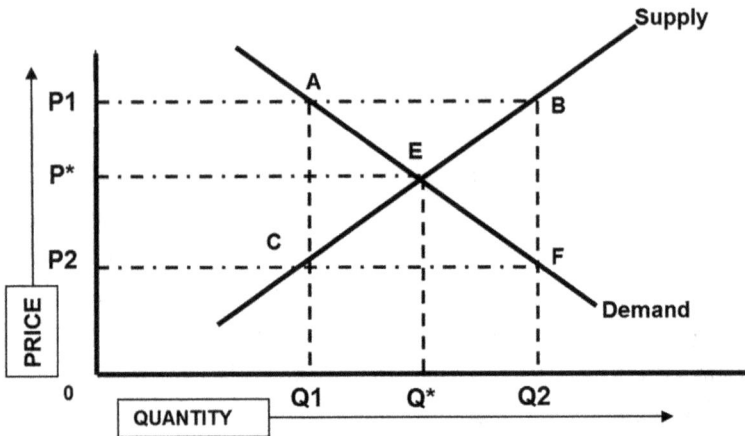

Explanation:

- The demand line represents the buying plans of a specific product.
- The supply line represents sellers of the product.
- Point E is the complete equilibrium between suppliers and buyers. This means that the demand for the product (quantity) lies on line Q*E and the price buyers are willing to pay is P*E. This is called the complete equilibrium between buyers and sellers.
- Now, let's assume that buyers are not interested in the product, and the demand is Q1A. What do you think will happen to the price? Alternatively, what happens if the demand becomes Q2B?

New entrepreneurs often do not understand this relationship and then overprice consumer goods and underprice industrial goods. This too can lead to business failure, as it will impact sales negatively.

When selling consumer goods, remember that they are generally lower-cost items and will be volume driven. The sales are not one-to-one sales. They are generally one-to-many sales. The salesperson is most often a cashier who simply takes payment. The consumer carries the cost of visiting the seller in order to select and buy the product; therefore, profit margins will be lower.

Industrial goods, which are generally sold to other businesses, involve a one-to-one sales process and often require the business to send a salesperson to visit the client as part of the sales process. The seller bears the cost of visiting each client independently and will therefore tend to sell goods with higher profit margins. These two thoughts on consumer and industrial goods are generalizations but can provide a useful guide.

Rainmaker Observation: For SMEs, it is imperative that the chosen strategy is not a price-based one. This is a poorly chosen strategy, whereas a niche market strategy is the most suitable. Although there may be exceptions, this is unlikely.

CHAPTER 10

Feasibilities

There are entrepreneurs who believe that the time it takes to complete feasibilities or due diligences risks the idea being stolen by competitors. The truth is that this may occur but it is better to have an idea stolen than to rush into implementing an idea that will be costly. There are times when critical dealbreakers are not immediately ascertained, which could result in financial ruin. In fact, you will find that funders always undertake their own feasibility, whether you have undertaken one or not.

This chapter thus highlights the following:

- Organizational and staff feasibility studies.
- Competitive analysis.
- In-depth market and financial feasibility studies.

In conducting a feasibility study, factors need to be identified and analyzed *before* an idea is implemented. In this chapter, *The Rainmaker* demonstrates how to assess the variables that may determine the success of such an idea and ultimately the business as a whole.

The normal process of feasibility is as follows:

- Define the issue (often called *the problem*) that you wish to review.
- Conduct research and international best practice identification on this issue.
- Undertake financial modeling and ratio analysis.
- Compare industry peers to your company or idea.
- Undertake scenario brainstorming sessions.
- Identify the most likely potential outcome of decisions made.
- Conduct follow-up evaluations.
- Make a final decision.

In feasibility studies, *the problem* is carefully set out in a formal document. The board's wishes and intentions are then documented . *The problem* and board wishes are then compared to the outcomes of the feasibility and are considered after in-depth discussions. This is followed by either a request for additional research or a decision made as to the steps to be undertaken for its implementation.

The feasibility study investigates and assesses information under three general categories:

Required info	Feasibility variables
Inputs	• Environmental inputs that influence *the problem* such as weather or geologic factors. • All inputs which you believe are necessary for *the problem* to meet a planned demand. • Categorized these as useful or not useful in effecting control of your systems.
Outputs	• Desired: the results of a process that meets management targets Not desired: The results of a process that has been negatively influenced (political, or socioeconomic) the results and thus targets.
Parameters	• These are established maximum and minimum expected results that are used to measure forecast capabilities of the existing market/product or service. • Ask: How will this change management strategy?

The total feasibility study can be broken down into six areas, which are discussed below.

Feasibility 1: Technical Viability

The aim of this feasibility is to determine whether your company has the resources to produce a product or service. In a technical feasibility study, the following factors need to be analyzed.

- Do you have competent and technically trained staff to produce the product or service?
- Do you have enough space and correct infrastructure to deliver the required product or service?

- Do you have the right machinery to produce the product or service?
- Have you carried out product design and quality standards?
  - Have you considered where this product and service will be based? Is it close to consumers and raw materials? Will it be easy to transport to your market?

Such a study should always be conducted before proceeding with a corporate strategy.

Feasibility 2: Organizational Structure Viability

Even if you have the best organizational structure that money can buy, it would be useless anywhere in the world if you don't have skilled and experience staff to operate within that structure. The obvious fault many entrepreneurs make is to attempt to carry out all the tasks themselves. This often results in burnout and failure. It is rather simple; your duty is to run the company and to appoint people who will undertake specific tasks for you.

Remember that your organization has specific goals to accomplish and this can only be achieved through research, which ultimately determines what the best and most reliable structure for your business is. Therefore, assess the following issues when undertaking an organizational viability study:

- Be specific about the type of organizational structure that you will need.
- Your structure must be flexible enough to account for future changes in the market.
- Assess the type of personnel needed, such as experience, skill, and seniority.
- Ask whether your board has enough experience to lead planned tasks.

It is at this point that critical decisions must be made. If the above two feasibilities are not positive, then the process must be stopped and reviewed to reassess the stated *problem*.

Feasibility 3: Analysis of Competition

Entrepreneurs being enthusiastic about launching a new product or even a new business is not uncommon. However, they need to take cognizance of competition and what they may do to influence the outcome of their launch and ultimately their profits.

This statement is relevant to companies that successfully launched products in the past. The essence is that your new product is not competition-proof, and you may become the target of either direct or indirect competition (or both):

Type of competition	Definition
Direct	Defined as the number of similar products and services offered in the same target market.
Indirect	Defined as potential entry of substitutes to compete with your product.

Given the basic economic principles of supply and demand, you are expecting to offer consumers a new product when their financials are already under strain. Always ask yourself this question: *Why should they change to your product?* Take note of the following:

- How many competitors are there in your industry, that is, the number of similar products already on the market and their respective market shares?
- How successful are these competitors, and will their strategies influence your proposed business?
- Do you have a competitive advantage? Ask yourself what your competitive edge is?
- What do you anticipate your competitors will do when you launch your product or company?
- Have you conducted a SWOT analysis on your competitors to identify possible weaknesses that may offer you opportunities to enter the market?
- How will you handle your competitors' strengths?
- Identify substitutes and assess potential influence on your profits from both local and foreign companies?

- Is the market large enough to absorb additional products without negative influences on profits?
- Are industry growth rates rising or falling?

As a starting point, use the following simple and useful technique to establish a competitor profile:

State the nature of your industry. There are generally four main categories, namely, mining, financial, property, and industrial.

Establish the major players within the industry and then do the same for your product.

Selecting a Competition Strategy

Selecting a competition strategy is difficult.

Porter's Five Forces (outlined in later chapters) states that only the top two or three players in the market are likely to have enough capacity to compete on price. This is particularly true for small and medium-sized enterprises (SMEs), which are often too easily copied. Pricing is critical and can be the defining activity that leads to failure or success. There is a tendency among SMEs to always try and compete on price, a strategy that cannot succeed.

The ideal strategy for SMEs is establishing a niche market; however, finding the correct niche and ensuring that it is large enough to support your growth strategy is a difficult part for many would-be entrepreneurs.

There are three rules to implementing sound niche market strategies:

- **Identify and meet market needs:** The promises you make to the market must have special appeal to consumers.
  - What can you provide that's new and compelling?
  - Identify the unique needs of potential buyers.
  - Can you alter your product or service to meet this expected demand?
  - A starting point could be to assess all product or service variations.
- **Understand your market:** When approaching a niche market, it's critical to have an in-depth knowledge of the product or service.
  - Essentially, you need to communicate to the niche audience information that will attract them to your product.
  - Consequently, market and sales must be well coordinated.

- **Conduct peer analysis:** Before moving further, assess direct competitors to determine what your competitive edge is and use that aspect to your benefit.
  - If you have no direct competition, assess why is it so. You may discover that other companies have tried and failed to launch similar products or services.
  - Conduct a thorough assessment of the market to test market receptiveness to the product or service; usually conducted through market surveys .
  - The bulk of SMEs try to compete, or intend to compete, on the basis of price and then wonder why so many of them fail.
  - As a funder, the best way to mitigate risk is to get the SME owner to think entrepreneurially and to focus on profit and not sales maximization.
  - SMEs can also allow the owner to be more entrepreneurial in the niche market than elsewhere. One can create a niche market and recreate it regularly as an entrepreneur. A niche market is conducive to developing and honing the entrepreneur's skills.

Note: One way to determine the competitors in any industry within a defined location is to look at the sectors listed in the country's stock exchange. These sectors set out the main competitors and will give you an extremely sound idea of the strength and size of the market and products sold. It will also provide you with statistics on the current business cycle.

Feasibility 4: Market Viability

The market viability study will inform whether there is sufficient demand on the market to make the launch of your business or product a success.

Rainmakers are often astounded by the lack of management's knowledge about the nature and size of the market, and they see this as a major reason why businesses run into trouble or even fail. The market feasibility study will help you to avoid getting into markets with little potential and will highlight the following:

- **Market potential:** potential customers, motivation and decisions to buy particular products, and reasons why they would change to your product.
- **Forecast:** potential market share, costs of entry, and ratios to achieve profits.
- **Break-even point:** Will your business be able to generate sufficient sales to break even within a predetermined timeframe?

Feasibility 5: Financial Viability

This study aims to assess whether the business or the launch of a new product will be financially viable.

It will enable you to determine whether your business can operate profitability and to calculate capital required, expected operating costs, and the timeframe to break even. Other variables determined include mark-up percentage, cash flow requirements, and anticipated profit. In fact, experts suggest that you start with the following:

- A calculation of your start-up costs.
- How you will finance these?
- Assessing the break-even point.
- Will funders wait for you to reach a profitability status?

Feasibility 6: Market Research

To reduce the risks of poor or uninformed business decision-making, systematically follow the steps listed here:

- What is the objective of the research?
- Define the target market.
- Collect data making use of the following:
  - Secondary sources (existing sources)
  - Primary sources (original research conducted by yourself or a contracted company).
- Assess and interpret the data.
- Brainstorm and draw conclusions.

The important starting point is to clearly define your target market. Being too general is pointless. This leads to excessive and too often expensive research. For instance, if you are a junior miner in the coal industry, with the aim of expanding operations, it would be useless to have your defined market as general mining.

In this example, the defined market would be coal, and the location would be the area to be expanded. However, this does not mean that general mining shouldn't be researched on to place the coal industry in context of the commodities cycle. In fact, all research should use the following systematic steps:

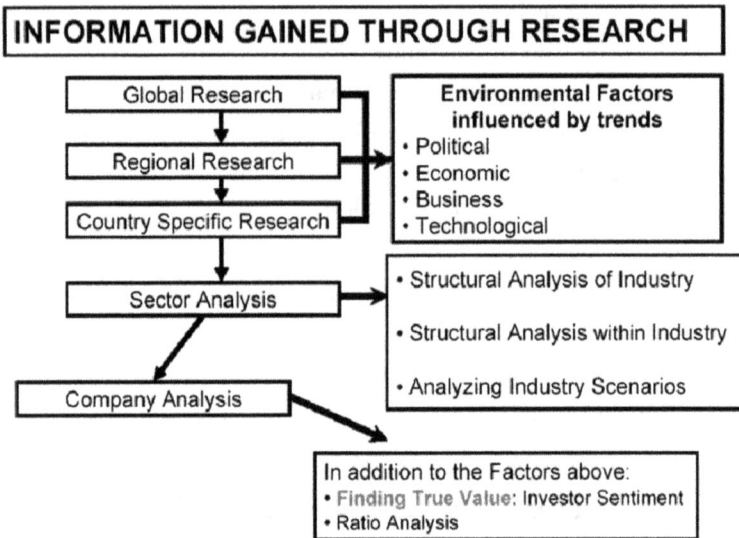

INFORMATION GAINED THROUGH RESEARCH

Global Research	→	**Environmental Factors influenced by trends** • Political • Economic • Business • Technological
Regional Research		
Country Specific Research		
Sector Analysis	→	• Structural Analysis of Industry • Structural Analysis within Industry • Analyzing Industry Scenarios
Company Analysis	→	

In addition to the Factors above:
• Finding True Value: Investor Sentiment
• Ratio Analysis

The idea is to gather information on global, regional, and local markets to be able to conduct structural analysis and subsequently find the true value of the industry. This places you in a more informed position to make relevant and ultimately profitable decisions.

To gage investors' and customers' sentiment, a survey should be conducted with a representative sample of the target population, which should be analyzed by statisticians. Data collection can also be done by using existing sources of media and research files, for instance, the World Bank, International Monetary Fund (IMF), or United Nations (UN).

Although useful, data gathered from secondary sources often are not specific enough to carry out structural analysis.

Be careful not to steer research arbitrarily. As such, conclusions must be fair and realistic.

Rainmaker Observation: The completion of research does not signal the launch of your company or product. First, you need to resolve the issues that have come up during the research, then you can reassess and launch.

CHAPTER 11

Who Are All These People?

Funders want to know more than just who the CEO is. They need to know that, if something happens to you, your team will be able to continue running your business, and that they will be able to do that as well as you can. This is the reason why selecting staff, from key personnel to directors, must be made for the good of the company, that is, by emphasizing on their qualifications, experience, skills, and their reputation.

Building Your Team

Every entrepreneur must learn to delegate, identify what tasks need to be done, and assign these to personnel. Almost every new business today uses consultants for the complex areas of research, law, audit, taxes, and insurance.

Management

Most capital providers will place a major emphasis on the skills and experience of the board of directors and key personnel. While your firm may be small when you are approaching these funders, remember that they are assessing your ability to run a much larger company in future. Why would you need capital if not to expand your business?

Rainmakers always look at your executive triparty team, namely, the CEO, the financial director, and the chairman. Your ability to show funders that together you form a powerful combination of leadership, industry knowledge, and financial discretion will be a major benefit to your organization, from capital raising to company control.

A range of other skills required to manage a business successfully include the ability to lead a group of employees; the ability to resolve conflicts arising among staff members, management team members and those between management and staff; and good communication skills.

Consultants and Professionals

The extent to which you employ professionals will depend on your own expertise, risks associated in the industry sphere in which you operate, and your goals for the business. The following aspects require due attention:

- How do I appoint the right consultants?
- Importantly, make sure that their expertise is both theoretical and practical.
- You will be working closely with these consultants, so ensure that your personalities don't clash.
- Assess their fee structure and compare this to what other consultants charge.
- Appoint financial accountants that have a background in auditing and forecasting.
- Build a legal team to resolve legal issues that may arise in the future.

Before the final selection of your team takes place, consider the following:

- **Personality:** Funders are concerned about their funds and your ability to pay them back, so obviously they want to feel comfortable that you have what it takes to be successful. Do this by highlighting your team's combined skills and experience to demonstrate that you have the ability to make your business a success.
- **Management:** Key personnel must display an understanding of your market and have the skills to succeed. Give detailed resumes of your management team, outlining in particular the vital roles they will play in the business' success. If your team can be stronger, take on the task of building up a team to support your own success as well as the success of your funding request.
- **Consultants:** Carefully select consultants who can help you. Know what it is you want in advance of your need to avoid delays.

- **Continuity:** Ensure that you have detailed and documented plans for your business so that it can continue to prosper even in your absence. Train someone to take over the firm and have keyman insurance in place considering the possibility of illness, disability or death. Funders will ask whether, without you, the business can continue to prosper.

Employing Staff

- In a world where labor-related laws have proliferated to protect employees from unscrupulous employers, you need to be more discerning when appointing staff. SMEs generally battle to comply with all the relevant legislation that pertains to employees and employment. For this reason, you must have employment contracts drawn up by an attorney specializing in labor law.
- You can also look to recruiting your staff through a reputable personnel agency. If you do not plan carefully at this stage you could face huge penalties in staff labor-related actions.

Employment and Termination Contracts

- These contracts are unique in every business and must be prepared by professionals.
- My advice is to review contracts annually to ensure it is up to date with any new legislation or changes to existing labor laws and legislation.
- Laws pertaining to dismissals or retrenchments are complex, and it is simply prudent to hire the right professional to handle such issues.

Treat Suppliers and Customers Like Staff

Suppliers

This can be a strange element to the success of your business. Once you have researched suppliers and made your selection based on price, quality and references ensure that these suppliers understand your specific needs.

The secret is to be loyal to a small group of suppliers to build relationships. Consequently, if a deal collapses or you have customers that haven't paid you, you can negotiate with your supplier to assist you.

Credit Customers

If you sell goods on credit, it is critical to ensure that your credit control systems are established and professional. This means that credit applications forms must comply with the laws of the land and that your systems can handle sales volume.

Strangely, a well-drawn credit application often results in clients paying on time if there are incentives via discounts and so on.

Social Media—More People to Know?

In today's electronic world, the quickest way to market your business is via networking, which is now critical to the success of your business. This is especially true if you are selling industrial products. Here too, you will need to hire professionals to truly understand the benefits of social media. At the outset, it is also important to note that social media highlights your business to competitors, and fake news and negative rumors are easy to start but difficult to defend.

Quite simply, social networking must be targeted and specific. Knowing many people doesn't equate to more business. Traditionally, networking is maximized when you join an organization such as the chamber of commerce. Here you get to meet members face-to-face, and deals are more definitive and potentially profitable. Remember, the idea is to meet people and not to get business, as people will automatically do business with those they like. Building contacts is important for now but even more important for the future.

Five Basic Steps

- **Step 1: Why network?** The aim is to promote your company, products, and brand. When the market gets to know who you are, your brand, in turn, gets promoted.

- **Step 2: Setting goals.** Brand specialists organize potential resources effectively to track and identify people, market leaders, and industries with whom you should connect.
- **Step 3: What network?** There are thousands of networking sites, and many cross the divide between personal and business; stay away from these sites. You are here to promote yourself to the business community, so stay on track. Be selective and specific as to the sites you choose to subscribe.
- **Step 4: Making contact.** Once the above steps have been completed, determine which organizations you wish to join and make contact. Sometimes you may be required to be referred by an existing member.
- **Step 5: Your approach.** The most appropriate approach depends on the organization, but the norm is the following:
  - Ensuring that calls are followed up and meetings organized and attended.
  - Promoting your organization's products and services.

Rainmaker Observation: To successfully run your business or to raise new funds, you must be able to demonstrate that you are consistent in achieving and succeeding in all that you do and, more importantly, that your staff are coordinated, happy, and faithful to your company. One-off successes may be impressive, but they are not enough to secure funding. In essence, do not leave things open to interpretation.

CHAPTER 12

Strategic Tools

Back to statistics. The global statistic is that more than 50 percent of companies' strategies only achieve 60 percent of their forecasted financials. And this is despite many of these companies taking consultants' advice to be conservative in their forecasts. Why is this?

Rainmakers suggest two reasons. First, company CEOs drive for growth when they actually need a more coordinated strategy. Second, when they do have a solid strategy, the execution of such a strategy is poor and ineffectual.

The Rainmaker looks at how to avoid these errors by viewing strategic planning and sales execution as inextricably linked. Both must rise in unison to achieve effective and real growth. The starting point to effectively manage both simultaneously is to continually apply straightforward rules, including the following:

- Keep your strategy simple and easy to implement.
- Follow your predetermined strategy as to resource allocation.
- Monitor performance as you implement sales strategy.

By following these rules, you reduce the potential to cause cash-flow shortfalls and have the ability to quickly identify strategic problems and to effectively make corrections.

Preferred Types of Strategies

Most entrepreneurs write business plans without basing their forecast and strategies on a sound foundation of research. As such, while you must set out your vision, mission, and goals, it is crucial to establish how these will be achieved within the environment you are operating. This includes three analytical strategies, namely, PESTEL analysis, Porter's Five Force analysis, and SWOT analysis. These three establish a solid foundation for the establishment of a business and an understanding of the environment within which the business will operate.

Three Strategic Methods

Strategy	Explanation
PESTEL analysis	• PESTEL stands for political, economic, social, technological, legal, and environmental. • It is used to assess the viability of your business within a broader economic environment.

Porter's Five Forces analysis	• An analytical model to analyze a company relative to its peers:
	  ○ Competitive rivalry
	  ○ Power of suppliers
	  ○ Power of buyers
	  ○ Threats of substitutes
	  ○ Threat of new entrants.

SWOT analysis	• SWOT stands for strengths, weaknesses, opportunities, and threats.

These three research methods enable you to establish how strong your business is compared to competitors' (Porter's), how strong it is relative to the market (PESTEL), and how it fares in an assessment of itself (SWOT).

PESTEL Analysis

This form of analysis is intended to provide you with an understanding of the external environment in which the business intends to operate, from the global markets to your more specific area of business. Many researchers tend to conduct PESTEL analysis to please management and funders. This is a complete waste of time and money. The analysis should highlight whether your company will prosper or fail within the market. Then take weaknesses and implement strategies to correct these.

Take cognizance of the following:

- **Political** factors highlight whether governments, or local authorities influence your specific industry with tariffs and country-specific area taxes. Under this heading you can add labor unions and their direct influence on your company that could have long-term negative or positive effects.

- **Social** factors assess cultural trends, demographics, population and socio-economic conditions.
- **Technology** factors pertain to changing trends that may affect the operations of the industry and the market via for instance new automation methods.
- **Legal** factors can be macro when laws are made or changed to a country or industry. Micro variables relate to laws that affect companies' structures.
- **Environmental** factors include all analyses of climate, weather, geographical location, and global changes in climate.

PESTEL analysis aims to identify major macroeconomic factors that have impacted or could in future impact your business and thus profitability.

Porter's Five Forces

Constituting what is called *Porter's Five Forces analysis,* the following factors are important to consider:

- **Strengths and Capabilities of Management:** Skills and capabilities of management and its team are important aspects to the ultimate success of your company.
  - ○ Each member of your team must be regularly assessed to establish how relevant, experienced, and skilled they are. These include the following:
    - ▪ Leadership ability.
    - ▪ Communication skills.
    - ▪ Vested interest in the business' success.
- **Ability to Sustain a Competitive Advantage**
  - ○ Funders are concerned that your company will be able to pay them back. As such, they are always interested in your company's ability to keep its competitive edge.
  - ○ Some variables to keep your edge are as follows:

- Ensure that your products and services have copyrights and patents.
- Continually implement marketing and promotional strategies to justify a higher price.
- Keep a check on supply–demand variables to assess demand trends. You should be looking for patterns that help you assess whether your product is at risk of becoming obsolete.

- **Differentiation**
  - Some products or services are inherently unique by technical or patent designs; others achieve uniqueness through marketing or by combining products and services.
    - Your product should have an inherent uniqueness.
    - You also must have excellent marketing abilities.
    - Your product and marketing skills should be your competitive edge in the market.
    - For a technical product, you must possess significant internal skills.

- **Barriers**
  - It is important to establish barriers of entry to prevent new entrants from copying your model. Simply put, the more the firms that enter your market, the less the chances you have to dominate it.
  - The following must be considered:
    - Is it expensive or difficult for customers to switch away from your offering?
    - Do you have proprietary and protected technology?
    - Do you have all the significant distribution channels locked up?
    - Can you significantly benefit from economies of scale?

- **Prominence of Your Company**
  - Small or start-up businesses often fail to consider the impact of larger companies currently selling or soon entering the same market.
  - Do you have an established presence in the market?
  - Does your company's founder have a positive reputation in the market?
  - Do you have brand recognition or other intangible assets?

SWOT Analysis

The point of this exercise is to identify only those items that are considered a possible strength or weakness in the context of the PESTEL analysis. The reality is that strengths and weaknesses are often relative to the environment at a specific time. Thus, strengths and weaknesses can fluctuate in response to environmental fluctuations. Today's strength could be tomorrow's weakness and vice versa. Once the strengths and weaknesses are matched to the environmental issues identified in the PESTEL analysis, the pertinent opportunities and threats can be identified.

In essence, a threat is an external, macroenvironmental issue that is likely to have a negative impact on your business because of insufficient funds or product strength to counter opposition. Similarly, an opportunity is an environmental issue that is likely to have a positive impact on the business because of internal strengths, such as management, marketing and product demand strength

The SWOT analysis should also highlight what steps need to be taken in the short, medium, and long term to offset threats. The following is an example of variables considered during a SWOT analysis:

SWOT variables	Criteria
Strengths	• Competitive strength compared to peers • Availability of resources and assets • Skilled and experienced CEO, board, and key personnel • Knowledge of products or services • Strong financial systems • A solid marketing plan • Location • Price, value, and quality • Processes, systems, and IT • Communications • Management succession plans
Weaknesses	• Gaps in management • Lack of strength against peers • Poor reputation • Weak financials • Cash flow under strain • Reliability of market data • Weak processes and systems

SWOT variables	Criteria
Opportunities	• Ability to take advantage of new opportunities • Competitors not fully aware of new opportunities • Technology development and innovation • Niche target markets • Strategies in place
Threats	• Politics, legislation, and environmental effects? • IT developments • Competitor intentions unsure • Market demand not fully established • Loss of key staff is a possibility • Economic growth remains uncertain

Application

Strategic Importance

	Most used tools	Most valued tools
Strategy Analysis	• SWOT • Porter's Five Forces • PESTEL	• PESTEL • Porter's Five Forces

Consultants and researchers use strategy tools to identify and implement organizational plans. In fact, in an increasingly competitive business world where the ability to spot new opportunities needs to be efficient and timeous, these kinds of tools are critical. The challenge for managers, however, is deciding which of these tools to use and when best to use them.

In exploring the use of strategy tools in organizations, the following was concluded:

- That there are 10 global strategy tools, namely, SWOT analysis, key success factors, core competences analysis, scenario planning, value chain, Porter's Five Forces, resource-based analysis, industry life cycle, PESTEL analysis, and portfolio matrices.
  ○ Strategy tools most used are Porter's Five Forces, SWOT, and PESTEL.
  ○ Scenario planning is more useful in strategy sessions to determine true potential market values of a company or product.
  ○ An analysis of key success factors tends to be used for strategy implementation.

- • However, there is a word of warning for Western economies and managers in general. Research highlights that business leaders in Asia, Africa, Middle East, or South America use a higher number of tools than managers from companies in Western countries, in the United States and Europe. This may have repercussions for the future competitiveness of Western firms in global markets.

Rainmaker Observation: It must be stressed that the foregoing tools are an integral part of the analytical entrepreneurial process of establishing a solid company structure and must be combined with feasibility studies.

CHAPTER 13

Isolating Start-Ups and Strategic Rules

The Rainmaker has a different approach to identifying critical success factors for start-ups from those success factors for established businesses. So before looking at general rules for strategy implementation, the difference between start-ups and established companies is highlighted.

Start-Ups versus Established Companies

Start-Ups

Summary of critical success factors for start-ups

Number	Description
1	Identify an opportunity.
2	Conduct market research.
3	What makes this opportunity different?
4	What strategy tool do you use to draft your business model?
5	What is your strategy?
6	Conduct feasibility.
7	Draft a business plan.
8	Carefully select and set up your business location.
9	Determine source of start-up capital.
10	Conclude, make a decision, and launch.

Note from the foregoing table that planning of business strategies forms the focus, which helps to emphasize the importance of such strategies and methods in the success of any new venture. In the table that follows, management skills and experience required for an established business are particularly highlighted and stressed.

Start-Up Costs

In addition to costs associated to running an established company, the following need to be considered for start-ups:

- Product development costs.
- Market research and development of the product idea.
- Legal costs for registration of the company and any intellectual property protection required, such as patents or trademarks.
- Cost of purchasing or leasing premises, including fixed assets.
- Office equipment.
- Provision for operating costs, among other:
  - Salaries and wages.
  - Rental interest.
  - Advertising.
  - Provision for unforeseen expenses.
  - Current assets, such as stock and debtors.

The initial calculation of the foregoing establishment costs will enable you to determine the total costs required to start your business. At this early stage you can then decide whether you have enough funds to start the business and/or whether you need bridging capital or long-term loans.

Established Firms

Summary of critical success factors for established businesses.

Number	Possess
1	Set out management skills or experience.
2	Establish strategic skills.
3	Establish technical skills.
4	Review your organizational structure.
5	Ensure financial management systems.
6	Promote leadership and communication skills.
7	Inventory and cash-flow management systems
8	Marketing and advertising skills.
9	Establish contingency plans.
10	Controls and systems.
11	Growth-orientated focus.

There is clearly a difference between what is important for start-up and established enterprises, and the entrepreneur and the funder both need to understand the shift that occurs as the business transitions from a start-up to an established company.

From a macroeconomic perspective, an entrepreneur's creativity is the driving force for development of new products or services and thus economic growth. In addition, dedication and determination to succeed drive the individual to achieve their goals. For the true entrepreneur, success is the motivator and profits are the reward.

To take the definition further, a successful entrepreneur tends to be one with leadership qualities. This is the ability to create rules and to set realistic goals. It is then their endeavor to follow through to see that their self-established rules are followed and goals accomplished.

Strategy Rules

Follow the Simple Basics

- **Keep it simple.** Avoid complex and drawn-out descriptions of goals. Just state what your company will accept and what it will not.
- **Challenge every decision.** Ensure that decisions influencing your long-term strategic plans reflect real market economics and your organization's actual performance relative to competitors'.
- **Communicate.** Unite all key players with strategy, marketing, and finance in a common communication framework for continually assessing performance.
- **Allocation of resources.** Business units should have a manager who communicates (before required) the need for additional resources required to execute their strategy.
- **Set priorities.** Delivering planned performance requires a few key actions taken timeously and effectively. Make strategic priorities and goals clear and unambiguous so that all key players know what and when to focus on implementation.
- **Monitor everything**. Use management systems to track results in real time and establish a timeline of results to set objectives.

This enables effective monitoring and, where need be, a strategy for cash flow involving a change in resources.

- **Execution.** Make selection and development of key managers a priority.

Rainmaker Observation: Every entrepreneur has these qualities in different degrees. While many of these skills can be taught, the innate desire to succeed seems to be the intangible quality that separates those who build on their successes and those who fail.

CHAPTER 14

Rainmaker Solving Tools

Decision-Making Tools versus Strategy

The simplistic way to define the difference between strategy and decision-making tools would be as follows:

- Strategic decisions are long-term, complex decisions made by CEOs, senior management, and board of directors.
- Tactical decisions are medium-term, less complex decisions made by middle managers.
- Decision-making tools aim to meet current objectives stated in strategic documents and plans.

As such, understand that decision techniques are critical to effective management.

Decision Making

Main Steps

- **Being specific:** In order to find the right decision-making tool, you need to be clear on the decision that must be taken.
- **Details:** Information is power, so gather all critical and relevant data pertinent to the task at hand, which can be conducted via questionnaires or discussion groups.
- **Alternatives:** Always take advantage of research to assimilate various options to help you make a decision.
- **Determination of options:** Once all data has been gathered and assessed, pick the option that suits the company's strategy and corporate direction.

- **Implementation and evaluation:** Once a decision has been made and reviewed, don't hesitate and take action to implement it and continuously monitor it until the final outcome. If desired results are not being achieved, review the decision and reevaluate. If need be, stop the process immediately.

The above steps are simplistic but do enable you to be practical in decision making. Over the years, this will add to managerial experience and skill, and will help your business to grow at a faster rate. The techniques in this section help you to make the best decisions possible with the available information. These tools help you assess the likely consequences of decisions, evaluate individual factors, and choose the best alternative actions.

The following techniques help to make decisions where there are many factors to consider.

Problem-Solving

Over the years, entrepreneurs have said that tools in this section have helped them to understand complicated situations and not just methods to make informed decisions. Without these tools problems nearly always seem overwhelming.

These techniques help you look at the multitude of variables in a structured and logical way, effectively giving you a starting point in problem-solving. The starting point is to extract information from facts and then to understand associated problems in detail.

There will always be far too many factors to consider and as such far too many issues to analyze. The way around this is to drill down this information to identify the possible causes of the problem or decision issue at hand. Drill down does help you to break large, seemingly unmanageable trends and problems down into achievable parts. It also helps you to see where you lack information. It is recommended that you understand how each fact relates to another, which can be done via SWOT analysis, financial forecasts, and risk-to-reward analysis.

- **Forecasting** shows you how to make financial models of your organization or new product launches. You can use these to work out whether projects are viable now or only in the future and ultimately use them to forecast the effects of changes in underlying factors.
- **Risk-to-reward** analysis establishes a framework for identifying the risks you face relative to forecasted profits. It also helps you to work out a strategy for controlling such variables.

Strategic Tools

Force Field

To carry out this analysis, follow these steps:

- Clearly describe your plan for a project. List all factors and potential changes to macroenvironmental factors that could influence your decision.
  - Assign a score to each force, from 1 (weak) to 5 (strong).

Pareto Analysis

To carry out this analysis, follow these steps:

- List the expected problems you could face.
- List the options that are available to you now and in the future.
- Apply an appropriate score to each option and then work on the option with the highest score.

Often better known as "the 80/20 rule," this method assists you to find where you can derive the greatest benefit by expending the least cost.

Paired Comparison

After assessing various options (the foregoing methods) you can now use paired comparison to relate and compare the best two options. For each comparison, decide which of the two options is most important and then assign a score to show how important they are.

Follow these steps to use the technique:

- List the two options you wish to compare.
- Assign a score to each element of the option.
- Evaluate a larger set of options based on numerous criteria, then weight the importance of each criterion to derive the best choice.
- Consolidate the results by adding up the total of all the values for each option.

Decision Trees

This method is an excellent tool for helping you to choose between several courses of action.

It enables you to investigate the possible outcomes of your decision. They also help you to form a balanced picture of the risks versus rewards associated with each possible course of action.

Plus, Minus, and Interesting (PMI)

PMI is a simply method of weighing the pros and cons, and implications of a decision.

When you have selected a course of action, check that your decision is worth taking. To use the technique, draw up a table with three columns headed Plus, Minus, and Interesting. Within the table write down all the positive points of following the course of action, all the negatives, and all the interesting implications and possible outcomes.

List all the pluses, minuses, and implications behind any decision, then assign a + or − numerical value to each based on your perception of the future. You are effectively identifying all forces for and against a theoretical change, weighted for amount of force exerted.

Cost–Benefit

Despite generating solutions to a problem and implementing these solutions in a rigorous manner the solution may still not be worth implementing. It may be that such implementation will be time-consuming and expensive.

Cost–benefit analysis is simple and often used by managers to decide-whether to implement a decision. To use the technique just add up the value of the benefits of an action and subtract the costs associated with it.

The techniques in this chapter help you to make the best decisions possible with the available information. With these tools you will be able to map out the likely consequences of decisions, work out the importance of individual factors, and choose the best course of action.

Rainmaker Observation: When you are overwhelmed with a deluge of available information, the tools described in this chapter help to filter information for you to decide whether a course of action is worth following. Do remember, though, that such tools are only to assist you to make logical and commonsense decision. They are not considered analytical enough for capital raising.

CHAPTER 15

No One-Size-Fits-All Strategy

Troubleshooting Internal Matters

The field of strategy has come under immense scrutiny over the past 20 years and in particular since 1997 when emerging markets crashed and changed the way companies conducted business. There is no doubt that continually shifting trends have repeatedly hit the global economy, to the point, in fact, that many theorists and market and industry experts have even come to question the viability of strategic thinking. Why, they ask, should one have a strategic division when strategy is continually changing?

Experience has shown that companies that follow trends ultimately never become winners. Those that have strategies in place lead the pack as trends do not change overnight. Therefore, entrepreneurs who have the foresight to have strategic plans in motion know that it is easier to change the direction of a strategy than to start one from scratch. The introduction of complex systems thinking in the late 1980s and early 1990s was a step in the right direction. However, there is still some way to go before companies' use of strategy become the norm rather than the exception.

Many smaller businesses believe that strategy simply means focusing on the company's core skills and products. Then, once they have achieved a level of comfort in the process of identifying their firm's core competencies, they develop a mission statement to make sure that the workers keep focused.

In reality, strategy is never that simple.

Contrary to popular belief, strategy may have nothing to do with a firm's core competencies. In fact, those who base a strategic plan on a firm's historical competencies do find themselves in trouble when global markets change, or they become the target of a hostile takeover. In the former, the company may find that they have started losing market share to the point where they can no longer compete. In a sudden corporate change (as in the latter), the company cannot focus on anything other than the corporate issue at hand. This type of trouble may be one of the reasons why some ignore strategy. With the apparent failure of strategic planning in the corporate sector, many questions have been raised. While researching and writing Jungle Tactics in 1997, I had to stop when emerging markets suddenly took a tumble. The lack of strategy was apparent in the failure of many firms to take action during that turbulent time. The book took another 3 years to complete, as research and new findings added new scope to the book.

A conclusion drawn from the *Jungle Tactics'* research is that companies that continually develop and execute sound strategy are significantly more profitable than those that do not. Analysis of companies that fail clearly reveal that their failure was caused by poor ability to determine changing needs of their target markets. As such, despite current thinking in many different areas of the field of management, corporate strategy is clearly the key to sustainable profitability in the new global economy.

Managers need to understand what does not work for firms as well as what does work. The field of strategy has encountered problems, not because corporate strategy itself has failed but because the wrong approach to strategy has been employed. Ultimately, strategy is simply and profoundly the foundation of the future profitability of firms. Managers who understand the practice will be much better prepared to lead the global organization in the early twenty-first century—in a time of change and uncertainty.

The counterargument to using strategic tools is that strategy itself seems to be in a state of confusion. With the multiple and, indeed, often contradictory strategic models available to managers, how would you effectively choose one model over another? In fact, some entrepreneurs have pointed out that several models can give you extremely different results. Today's strategists state that it is critical to understand the nuances of tools available and what the results actually imply. It is also worth noting that the greatest use of strategic tools is at the micro-company stage, whereas at small and medium-sized enterprise (SME) stage this reduces and further falls during the established stage of a company's cycle.

The reason for this may be that companies in the first stages of their development tend to be very dynamic and therefore need to use more strategic tools to make sense of the environment in which they are competing. Additionally, companies in their start-up stages may have to spend more time designing their strategies or developing business plans in order to convince investors.

Industry Type

Amazingly, it is not just large established firms that use strategic tools. In fact, it is more pertinent to look at the types of industries rather than the size of companies. For instance, power utilities, technology, media and information, and manufacturing companies use more strategic tools than companies in financial services.

Research indicates that, in fact, strategic tools tend to be used in sectors that are complex and competitive, and face both global economic challenges and local regulatory legalities. For instance, media and power utilities are industries that are highly regulated and thus require to continually present strategic analyses to regulators and other stakeholders as part of their required transparency. Interestingly, public, consulting, and professional companies use fewer strategic tools, which reflects the different competitive environments and the value that the public place on these organizations.

Final Comment on Strategy Tools

SWOT, Porter's Five Forces, and PESTEL have significantly greater use in strategy analysis than in any other stage. As such, these are preferred by consultants and managers alike for analysis and evaluation purposes.

Scenario planning, resource analysis, portfolio matrices, and industry life cycle tools are used for strategy choice. These are preferred methods by managers when they are making strategic choices.

A study of key success factors is the only tool used in implementation than in any other stage.

Rainmaker Observation: The use of strategy tools is at a lower level in strategy implementation. This does suggest a lack of tools oriented to implementation purposes or that professionals and managers do not give as much value to this stage of the strategy process.

CHAPTER 16

I Can't Find a Solution

Some businesses—no matter its size or industry—are inherently difficult to find a solution when problems arise. *The Rainmaker* can see the problem—a fall in sales or management ineptitude—but the true issue is to find a reason for such a problem and thus find a solution to resolve the problem. In today's complex mesh of cross-border business, varying language and cultural barriers, different corporate and state laws and forex intricacies, it can be a daunting task to find where the problem lies,which is the starting point. Once *The Rainmaker* find the problem and reason for the cause in the first place he or she still have to establish the right strategy to resolve the problem, which could be poor management decisions, technical difficulties, and inadequate financial systems to correct undesired financial outcomes.

In numerous instances, a concise course of action to resolve identified problems is not easily determined, and *The Rainmaker* is called in to conduct troubleshooting methodologies.

This chapter looks at some methods to help you to identify possible solutions. It must be stated that human behavior does tend to complicate the identification and implementation that is required to find solutions. There are many times when a simple error in judgment caused the mistake, but managers try and cover up their error, which makes it difficult (and costly) for *Rainmakers, who do not take shortcuts,* to resolve the problem.

Note that, given the vastness of this topic, we are limiting troubleshooting to financial difficulties.

Identifying the Problem

The financial performance of any business can be assessed using three well-known concepts: profitability, liquidity, and solvency.

Profitability

This is the most important determinant of your company's long-term business success. In the long run, managers must earn a competitive return on these contributed resources if the business is to continue to prosper and expand. They need to continually assess the relative cost of sales, factors influencing gross profit margins, interest rates, tax rates and level of depreciation.

However, without short-term strategies and cash-flow management, there is no long term. Effectively, managers need to balance strain on cash flow with proposed plans to launch new products. In the short run, managers must earn returns to pay for variable costs, and, if not possible, then short-term solutions are needed to avoid supplier or customer legal actions.

Liquidity

Liquidity refers to a business' ability to pay short-term debt

While profitability and liquidity are related concepts, many make the mistake to assume that they are the same. Unlike profit, cash flow includes loan repayments but does not include profitability factors such as depreciation, revalued inventory, or capital gains and losses.

Liquidity is thus best measured with cash-flow statements.

Solvency

Solvency refers to the ability of your business to manage debt during adverse economic and market conditions. In fact, it is synonymous with owner equity. From a *Rainmaker* point of view, the latter serves as a source of security when acquiring debt capital during difficult economic conditions. *The Rainmaker* always looks at the factors that influence the company's debt (gearing) ratio.

Solvency also indicates your business' risk-bearing ability and is measured using a balance sheet.

Potential Causes

To make matters worse, businesses find themselves in that predicament for more than one reason. Consultants, together with forensic auditors, will tell you that it is rare to find a situation where financial problems are caused by only one error. While financial difficulties tend to result in weakening profitability, liquidity, or solvency, the underlying cause generally tends to be associated with poor (or falling) efficiency, economy of scale of the business, and debt structure.

Efficiency

Efficiency refers to the direct relationship between sales and associated costs. So if efficiency is falling then the ratio is simple. Either sales are not rising at a greater rate than input costs or input costs are rising faster than sales.

However, *Rainmakers* will explain that there are no perfect measures of efficiency, which, to a large extent, is determined by managerial and technical skills. In larger operations, efficiency will reflect the performance of the owner as well as hired managers and workers.

As such, companies with low efficiency generally will show below-average profitability and results into losses. Improving efficiency, in the majority of cases, requires improving basic management and technical skills.

This is not easy. Ultimately, to better efficiency requires improving how you allocate your resources among different products and projects, and how organized and motivated your employees are to achieve set goals.

Economies of Scale

Scale refers to the opposite extremes of a company's size, too large or too small.

In large or complex companies, raw material or resource input can be spread too thinly, while small firms may have higher production costs per unit, as fixed costs are also taken into account. *The Rainmaker* also assesses labor requirements and compares this to the existing labor supply in the area within which the company operates. In addition to labor, give allowances for the company's use of external experts and consultants.

The Rainmaker also assesses and analyzes sales per worker. If labor costs are in excess to that required by a business, wages will adversely affect the profitability and liquidity of the business. If the scale of a business is inadequate, that is, this time the firm is too small relative to its labor supply, a number of options can be considered.

- The labor supply can be reduced through off-business employment.
- Labor utilization can be increased through expansion.

Debt Structure

This refers to the amount of outstanding debt, term, and cost to the company. While the norm is that firms run into financial problems when their debts are excessive, it can also be a problem when they have too little debt. The latter limits its size, efficiency, growth, and earning capacity.

Debt structure influences the following:

- Profitability through interest costs.
- Liquidity through debt servicing requirements.
- Solvency through the value of the assets available to secure the firm's liabilities.

Some debt structure problems are relatively easy to resolve, for instance, by lengthening loan terms to improve cash flow. *Rainmakers* are called in when debt structures involve adjusting the asset or liability structure of the business.

Usually as a last resort, CEOs will sell assets to reduce interest liabilities. Or they will sell assets that have debt service requirements in excess of their cash-generating potential. Adjusting debt structure usually requires a negotiated settlement between the borrower and the lender.

Rainmaker Observation: The first step in financial troubleshooting is to identify the type of problem that the firm is experiencing. If the problem is one of profitability, liquidity, or solvency, a strategy is established. Only an analysis of the environmental factors relative to income statements, cash flows, and balance sheets can establish the true weaknesses of a business.

CHAPTER 17

Not Standing Still

In an increasingly competitive global business environment, a manager's ability to identify and seize new opportunities, then strategize to plot a growth path for an organization and to use resources effectively and efficiently, becomes paramount.

There is a vast array of management tools available to meet such challenges, including tools for dealing with strategy analysis, decision making, and implementation. The challenge for managers is knowing which and when to use these tools. These have been discussed in previous chapters, so this chapter looks at rules to follow when your business is expanding.

Pre-expansion Rules

Once you have launched your business, you will quickly realize that to increase profits you will have to face the challenge of expanding your business. However, success to growing your business is dependent on first establishing a solid and profitable platform from which to launch growth strategies.

Entrepreneurs should take the opportunity to learn and gain skill and experience from all aspects of starting and running a business. Being involved in the daily operations will enable you to detect weaknesses as they arise and draft workable strategies to resolve such weaknesses. Understanding the basics and the very essence of what makes your business successful is critical for management to lead the business in future. Remember that in future you will be delegating tasks to newly employed managers. You will need to be able to describe what is required of them to make those divisions successful.

The Pilot Operation

There are some basic reasons why so many entrepreneurs ignore the importance of having a successful pilot operation in place before expanding. While the main factor stated by management is usually cost of running a pilot without income, the true factors tend to be overconfidence

The latter is self-explanatory. Not launching a product is a potential loss of sales and thus profits. The real problem is that managers are often overconfident in their abilities and their belief in their product. A possible reason for this is that many entrepreneurs have been successful in different or unrelated fields.

Another enemy is the dire panic to get to market first.

The Expanding Business

Taking your company to the next level takes planning and careful preparation. You will need more skilled staff, to whom you will need to delegate responsibility and authority. Where needed you will have to set up training to develop new and required skills for your expanded business.

Delegation of authority can be accomplished by adopting the following:

- Financial motivation of key employees.
- Creation of profit centers and share option schemes.

It is a normal for entrepreneurs of start-ups to find it difficult to delegate authority and as a consequence relinquish some control of their firms. This situation can be avoided, as there are ways to do so without giving up certain functions that you may want to keep control of. For instance, you can keep control of resource allocation and expense payments.

There are, in turn, two main ways that you can motivate key staff, namely, recognition for their work and commensurate reward for success. The most important recognition is to let staff know that they are in positions of authority as well as responsibility. Interestingly, this concept means that by delegating authority your managers' mistakes will be limited to their spheres of responsibility.

Key managers are best motivated by cash incentive plans that are linked to their specific success and not that of a group. While you are trying to build a team, it is only such compensation that will see managers strive to succeed. The other side of the coin is when managers fail in their responsibilities. There are also some basic rules to handling such problems.

Handling Serious Issues

- Start with identifying that there is in fact a problem.
- Get the manager responsible to acknowledge that there is a problem. Get them to write a report to explain irregularities.
- Immediately place the deal on hold. Even if the project is cancelled, you must cut costs immediately to safeguard positive cash flow and profitability.
- As the CEO, take responsibility and initiative to explain to creditors that there is a problem and you will keep them informed.
- Take action against managers responsible (if need be) and action to limit losses and exposure to market reaction.
- Look for opportunities in such moments of adversity.

One method to limit the effects of a specific project loss is to diversify in numerous regions or types of businesses.

Rainmaker Observation: Before expanding your business, you should consult your lawyer and forensic auditor to develop benefits for your future employees. The goal is to expand, which comes with more employees and managers. Look at the implementation of share and profit incentive schemes which are then included in your forecasts and budgets.

CHAPTER 18

Finances and Your Business

Facts of Life

Before you do anything, look at the following table for some age-old wisdom.

1	The golden rule ALWAYS applies: *He who controls the money rules*
2	Ultimate success is logic, clear understanding, and a strong grasp of market niche, your business, and industry. When running your business, a successful plan combines salesmanship and hard facts in an organized and logical manner. The success formula is *Information* ✕ *Competence* + *Energy* = *Success*
3	Irrespective of the type of financing you need, the process of obtaining it is usually the same. A finance plan will help you to profile the business and be helpful to the business owner and your investors, or prospective investors.

Some Thoughts

Consider the following:

- **What funds do you require?** This can only be calculated by serious cash flow planning, which requires forecasts of future sales, related costs, and capital and interest funding payments, depending on the type of capital you have raised.
- **How will you spend these funds?** Will you buy equipment, pay for expansion plans, appoint additional employees, research and development or for development costs?
- **Why should we lend you money?** One of the primary reasons businesses often fail is lack of managerial experience and skill to properly use funds as they are intended. You will need to convince investors, new directors, and key staff that you have the knowledge,

experience, and skill to manage your business and the funds that you have raised. And you will also to prove that you will achieve the forecasted profits.

- **What are the supply–demand variables for where your business operates?** Even if your business has a great growth potential, if the local economy is slow and restricted with exchange controls and other legislation and rules to the point that it is likely to impede your venture, you will find it difficult to raise funds.

- **Do you have strong financial systems in place?** The starting point for new businesses is to hire an external bookkeeper to work for you on a periodical basis. As sales and expenses increase as your firm expands, create an internal accounting department, overseen by a financial director.

Financing Your Business

How Much Do You Need?

Simply stated, total cash required is equal to the cost of fixed assets (land, buildings, machinery, etc.), plus start-up expenses, which include operating costs, inventory, and accounts receivable. It is important for all businesses to estimate capital requirements to ensure there is sufficient cash available to pay expenses as they occur.

Financial Projections

Find the latest costs for the following:

Item	Assess
Start-up	• Installation of power utilities. • Marketing and promotional materials. • Legal fees for incorporation.
Fixed assets	• Land, buildings, machinery, equipment, and vehicles. • Leasehold improvements. • Deposits on leases and utilities.
Inventory required	• Determine how fast you must pay your suppliers. • What percent of total accounts payable is to be paid in the month incurred? • What percent of total accounts payable is to be paid in 30 days, 60 days, etc.?

Item	Assess
Monthly sales	• Estimate sales for each product and service individually. • If part of your sales is on credit, estimate the delayed impact on cash flow.
Monthly expenses	• Rent. • Insurance. • Power utilities. • Salaries and wages. • Marketing, advertising, and promotions. • Legal and accounting fees. • Loan payments.
Financing your business	• Who will you approach to raise capital? • Decide whether you will require equity or debt financing? • Bank loans generally require the following: ○ A business plan. ○ Part personal investment (usually 10–30% of the loan amount). ○ Enough assets to collateralize the loan (usually 1–2 times the loan). ○ Good character and personal credit. ○ Personal guarantee (Your personal assets will be at risk.).

Funds to Start a Business

There are two basic sources of funds to start a business, namely equity and debt. Equity is an investment in the business by you or by a partner. Debt can be derived from private sources such as family and friends or from more formal sources, such as banks, capital providers, venture firms, and angels.

The more formal sources of funding will depend on how much you require.

- The amount of funds that you need and how it will be used. This is often determined by the industry that you are operating in.
- Your personal financial situation.
- How much collateral you have?
- Your managerial profile, history, and past successes.

Most start-ups don't start with bank loans or venture capital but launch their businesses with a combination of personal resources and help from family and friends. In addition, only a small number of start-ups begin with a bank loan and even less with venture capital.

For entrepreneurs who have little cash, personal assets, and bad personal credit, bank loans will be turned down. The only option is to approach equity partners, such as angel investors.

Type of Funding Available

Debt versus Equity

Debt funding is normally cheaper and easier to find than equity funding.

- **Debt Financing:** It carries the liability of monthly interest and capital payments, whether or not you have positive cash flow. Such financing is usually available to all types of businesses.
- **Equity** investors expect little or no return in the early stages but require much more extensive reporting as to the company's progress. They have invested in you and your promises, so they anticipate that goals and milestones will be met. As such, equity is usually focused on businesses with a fast and very high growth potential.

If you decide on debt financing, ask yourself the following questions:

- Does my company qualify for debt financing?
- What does this entail?
- How much debt can I afford?
- How will repayments work?
- What happens if cash flow is impacted?
- What happens if interest rates rise?
- Am I willing to be a guarantor and place personal assets at risk?

The following equity considerations should be made:

- What type of investors should do I approach?
- What can I sell shares for?
- Will this value to fair?
- If I do all the work, should I share control and future profits?
- Do I really want investors as partners forever?
- What stake in my company shall I sell?

Investors will want to take a much larger share of a start-up venture than they will of an established company with a profit history.

Angel Investors

Angels are individual private investors who make up a large portion of "informal" venture capital, who tend to invest small amounts ($25,000 to $250,000). Depending on how much you require, you may need to approach an angel. Beware of consultants who charge up-front fees to connect you with investors.

Venture Capital

Venture capital firms will only invest in companies with an expected high growth, and they will only do this by taking a very large stake in your business, sometimes as much as 75 percent of your shares.

Strategic Partnerships

Where two companies have a mutual benefit in setting up a strategic partnership, there is usually a parallel, such as one having the funds to invest and the other the market knowledge or plan. Another example is when one party has the product and the other the means to distribute that product via its network.

Government Small Business Loans and Funds

While this is a tremendous resource, these are usually time-consuming and filled with red tape.

The way these usually work is that firms leverage their private capital into government money to form a sort of venture capital fund to offer both long-term loans and equity participation. They tend to invest mainly in established companies for management buyouts, funds to list on an exchange, strategic partnerships, and bridge financing.

Commercial Papers

These are short-term debt instruments and usually issued for a period of 2 to 270 days. These come in the form of a promissory note that is unsecured and discounted from its face value.

The way it works is that the issue is usually backed by a letter of credit or a credit guarantee. The company may pledge assets to obtain a credit guarantee that is then leveraged into an issue of commercial paper.

Letters of Credit

These are issued to your funding source as a guarantee that you will pay for their services. So if you are not able to pay, the issuer will pay on your behalf. Your bank might issue a letter of credit (L/C) based on your pledge of a receivable or other fixed asset.

Receivable Factoring

Funds are advanced against goods sold and accepted, but funds have yet to be received. Normal advances on accounts receivable are 80 percent to 90 percent. The lenders are looking for ninety days or less to be paid. Funding is available for older accounts receivable, but the rates take a dramatic turn upward.

Purchase Order Advances

If you have purchase orders with your customer base, you may be able to get financial advances toward their completion. The typical advance is less than 50 percent, and the rates are very high.

Equipment Leasing

This is effectively renting assets that you need such as equipment and agree to pay rent for a specific period of time. There is no interest rate, but the rates tend to be higher than commercial loans. Some of this is offset by being able to expense 100 percent the payments.

Asset Sale Leasebacks

Simply put, you sell your assets and lease these back to continue your operations. The downside of this approach may be capital gains or sales tax.

Private Placements

You can raise capital by selling part of your company's shares to few private investors. Remember that you are effectively selling a part of your business, which also means that you are losing future value and, possibly, control.

Stock Market Listing

There are various forms and methods to list a company on an exchange, from small and medium scale enterprises (SME) exchanges to main boards across the world. These follow strict protocols that must be adhered to and can only be done by registered stockbrokers.

Limited Partnerships

This is another way of having a silent partner, who finances the company, while you take total responsibility to run the operations. There are numerous limited partnerships in the general public domain that have been formed to invest in businesses.

Convertible Debt

This is normally a loan that can be converted into an equity stake in the company. Ensure that there is a timeframe and value attached to this instrument.

Government or State Bonds

Most governments have revenue bonds that are designed as debt instruments, where the company issues the bond and a government agency underwrites it. These bonds are generally issued to promote manufacturing facilities that will create jobs.

Lines of Credit

These funds are available as drawdowns against the total line of credit and are most commonly secured with accounts receivable and inventory as collateral.

Negotiating Your Deal

The first lesson to learn is to say **NO**.

Most entrepreneurs approach the issue of negotiating with great stress, which leads directly to weak negotiations and a less-than-beneficial result. In order to avoid this from happening to you, take note of the following:

- Determine what you are negotiating for.
- Express what you are offering and want in return.
- Get it in writing.
- Leave nothing to verbal agreements.
- Relate everything to your long-term goals.
- Pay close attention to deal breakers.
- Establish what is acceptable and what is not.
- Ensure that there are no penalty clauses.
- Ensure that you have first option to buy back your stock at a fixed price.
- Pay attention to covenants, conditions, ratios, restrictions, or other clauses that can have serious long-term effects.
- Try to avoid pledging personal collateral. You may need these assets in the future to raise additional capital.
- Seek professionals before you sign. Lawyers and accountants can help spot details that may burden you in future.

Closing the Deal

Remember you are out there selling yourself and your company. Only accept "No" as being one step nearer to **Yes**.

Amount Requested

The simple rule is to get it right the first time. If you underestimate what you require and have to go back to investors, it will be looked on with disapproval. The fact is that if you can't estimate what you need how can you be trusted to use the funds effectively.

- **Conservative request:** Ensure that financial projections are based on a sound foundation of research that fully supports the amount of funds that you are requesting. If you are seeking debt financing your request must be specific. Investors may be inclined to stop financing your business if you can't make the funding work.

- **Downside planning:** In addition to correct forecasts and loan requirements, make sure that you take account of possible market anomalies that can cause temporary downsides and a slowdown in sales. It is far better to overestimate your capital requirements than to run short and be forced to return to investors.

- **Assumptions:** Both lenders and investors are going to want to know that you have reasonably estimated and supported your costs and projected revenues. Your financial forecasts should be linked to international best-practice research and ratios.

The Terms

Know what you want, what you can afford, and what you will give up.

- **Timeframe:** This should be linked to the useful life of the asset being financed. Receivable and contract financing are less than 1 year; equipment 1 to 5 years; and real estate and other long-term assets 5 to 20 years.

- **Amortized versus interest only:** Many ventures can take up to 18 months to reach breakeven before it starts to make money. Think about an initial period of interest only, or skip payments to help bolster cash flow.

- **Interest rate:** The rate that you pay for the funds that you need can directly affect your profitability, so negotiate a rate below the prime interest rate, thus giving you a buffer against unexpected market changes in rates. This may be fixed or free floating and depend on the country in question.

- **Penalties:** Funding sources are in control, and having spent time and money selecting deals to invest in, they will often insist on prepayment penalties to insure you'll leave the funds in place.

- **Blanket loans:** This will restrict your ability to raise cash in the future from alternative sources. Always attempt to have specific loans and not blanket ones.
- **Personal guarantees:** How committed are you? If you won't sign personally, then you may not get any money. If you don't believe in your success, why should anyone else? As you and your company begin to perform, you should be able to get these guarantees released.
- **Covenants:** These spell out just what you can and cannot do—no management or ownership change, regular filing requirements, no alternative sources of funding, deposits maintained, collateral pledges, and so on. Carefully read and evaluate the fine print.
- **Selling a stake:** What's fair? You must define it, support it, and defend it. While most lenders won't ask, most investors will demand.
- **Stock repurchase:** Negotiate an escape clause that will allow you a way out if you need it or can afford it. Ensure that you have the option to buy your stock back at a predetermined price.
- **Management controls:** Most entrepreneurs make decisions for the company to achieve its goals and ultimately profits. Some investors insist on participating in the decision-making process. Know what you are looking for and what you are willing to give up.
- **Collateral, anyone?** Will you risk it all? If you don't believe, neither will anyone else.

Rainmaker Observation: With investors, because there is no debt, they are concerned with profit margins and retained earnings. The projections should support ratios of better than 2.0 to 1 to generate any serious investor interest.

CHAPTER 19

Financial Forecasts

If you're thinking of starting a business or expanding an existing company, you'll need funds to finance the cost. This chapter hones down what it is you will require to launch your concept. So take a deep breath as we move into more strict rules of financial analysis.

To build an effective financial strategy to raise capital you should answer these questions:

- How much money do you need to launch a company or finance expansion?
- What are your timeframes?
- Do you need the following?
  - Additional fixed assets (machinery, property, or equipment and machinery).
  - Professional research and development.
  - Additional working capital.
- Where will these finds come from?
  - Personal or your own business.
  - Commercial banks and other conventional lenders.
  - Risk capital investors.
- Which option is best for you?

Projection Information

There is no option to raising funds. You must be able to present a clear, concise, logical, and financial projection backed by research. This is the most important key to having a chance of obtaining the capital you desire. If you don't have financial forecast ability, hire a researcher to obtain the statistics you desire to back financial forecasts and a forensic auditor to conduct financial projects using these statistics.

Note that your forecast should be set out monthly for the first year and annually for the next 4 years and should include notes to fully support the following:

- Sales estimates and related costs.
- Administrative, production and other costs.
- Indirect costs of sales.
- Inventory costs and turnover.
- Capital expenditures.
- Gross margin.
- Annual sales growth rates.
- Interest rates on debts.
- Income tax rate payable.
- How you intend to collect accounts receivable.
- Accounts payable schedule.
- Depreciation and amortization schedules.
- Usefulness of assets.

The Income Statement (Profit and Loss)

Income projections enable you to develop a forecast of expected income to be generated each month and for the business year, based on reasonable and fair predictions of monthly levels of sales, costs, and expenses.

Total Net Sales (Revenues)

The total number of products or services that you realistically expect to sell each month at prices based on market research. Use this step to create the projections to review your pricing practices.

Estimate the returns, allowances, and markdowns that you expect, given market trends.

Cost of Sales

The key to accurately calculating your cost of sales is take all costs into account to determine total net sales. Where inventory is involved, remember transportation costs and any direct labor.

Gross Profit

Subtract the total cost of sales from the total net sales to obtain gross profit.

Gross Profit Margin

The gross profit is expressed as a percentage of total sales and is calculated by dividing the gross profits by the total net sales.

Controllable Expenses

These include the following:

- Salary and wage expenses, including overtime.
- Payroll expenses, including sick leave, health insurance, unemployment insurance, and social security taxes.
- Outside services, including subcontracts, overflow work, and special once-off services.
- Supplies, including services and items purchased for use in the business.
- Repairs and maintenance, including regular maintenance and repairs.
- Advertising, including targeted classified directory advertising expenses.
- Car delivery and travel, including charges if personal car is used in business, including parking, tools, and buying trips.
- Accounting and legal, including professional services.
- Utilities costs.

Fixed Expenses

These include the following:

- Rent of business premises.
- Depreciation and amortization of capital assets.
- Insurance, including fire or liability on property or products and workers' compensation.

- Loan repayments, including interest on outstanding loans.
- Licenses and permits.
- Miscellaneous, which tend to be small expenditures without separate accounts.

Income Statement Worksheet

Revenue Projection

Step 1: Calculate turnover less expenses directly related to the sales.

- Total sales = number of credit and cash sales. Also called turnover and revenue.
- Total sales less costs of sales = total net sales
- This is also called gross profit.
  - Gross profit as a percentage of sales = gross profit margin (%)
    - This also denotes how productive a company is, in two ways:
      - **Relative to itself over the years.** If the ratio improves, the company is getting more efficient.
      - **Relative to other similar companies.** If your ratios are better than competitors, your system is more efficient and ultimately places you in a position to outperform competitors, but if you are not, take note and assess how you can improve these ratios.
        - As this is a ratio, the solution is either that your costs are too high relative to sales or that your sales are too low to justify costs.

Step 2: Calculate gross profit less expenses

- Controllable expenses include the following:
  - Salaries and wages.
  - Legal and accounting.
  - Advertising and promotions.
  - Vehicles.
  - Office supplies.
  - Power utilities.
  - Other.

- Fixed expenses include the following:
  - Rent.
  - Depreciation.
  - Insurance.
  - License and permits.
  - Loan payments.
  - Other.
- The foregoing two equal total expenses.
- Gross profit less expenses = profit before tax.

This form should be used to project monthly income and expenses for year I and then to provide annual projections for the next 4 years.

The Balance Sheet

Assets versus Liabilities

Step 1: Outlining Assets   List anything of value that is owned or legally due to the business. Total assets include all net values. These are the amounts derived when you subtract depreciation and amortization from the original costs of acquiring the assets.

- **Current Assets** include the following:
  - **Cash:** List cash and resources that can be converted into cash within 12 months from the date of the balance sheet.
    - Includes cash on hand and demand deposits in the bank.
  - **Accounts receivable:** The amounts due from customers in payment for products or services.
  - **Stock:** includes raw materials on hand, work in progress and all finished goods, either manufactured or purchased for resale.
  - **Investments:**
    - **Short-term Investments:** These include interest receivable and dividend income.
    - **Long-term Investments:** These include **shares**, bonds, and savings accounts earmarked for special purposes.
  - **Prepaid expenses:** goods, benefits, or services a business buys or rents in advance.

- **Fixed Assets include the following:**
  - ○ **Land, buildings, machinery, and vehicles:** List original purchase price without allowances for market value.
  - ○ **Improvements to property.**

Step 2: Outlining Liabilities

- **Current Liabilities**
  - ○ **Accounts payable:** Amounts owed to suppliers for goods and services purchased in connection with business operations.
  - ○ **Notes payable:** The balance of principal due to pay off short-term debt for borrowed funds. Also includes the current amount due of total balance on notes whose terms exceed 12 months.
  - ○ **Interest payable:** Any accrued fees due for use of both short- and long-term borrowed capital and credit extended to the business.
  - ○ **Taxes payable:** Amounts estimated to have been incurred during the accounting period.
  - ○ **Payroll accrual:** Salaries and wages currently owed.
- **Long-term Liabilities**
  - ○ **Notes payable:** List notes, contract payments, or mortgage payments due over a period exceeding 12 months. They are listed by outstanding balance less the current position due.

Step 3: Calculating Owners' Equity

- Also called net worth, it is the claim of the shareholders on the assets of the business. In a proprietorship or partnership, equity is each owner's original investment plus any earnings after withdrawals. In a corporation it is the capital investment paid for the issuance of stock, plus the surplus paid in by the principals, and the after-tax retained earnings.

Total Liabilities and Net Worth: The sum of these two amounts must always match that for total assets.

Cash-Flow Projections

A cash-flow model should have monthly details for the first year of operations, followed by a summary overview of how cash flow will be in the next 4 years.

Step 1: Cash and Cash Receipts

- Start with the cash you have at the beginning of the month, called cash brought forward.
- Add cash received from cash sales.
- Add collections from credit accounts.
- Add other cash injections.
  - This equals total cash receipts.

Step 2: Cash and Cash Payments

- Start with cash purchases.
- Add gross wages.
- Add payroll expenses.
- Add other, which includes advertising, office supplies, power utilities, sick leave, insurance, repairs and maintenance, taxes, travel and delivery services, and unemployment insurance.
  - This subtotal indicates cash payments for operating costs.

Step 3: Additional Cash Payments

- Loan principal payment.
  - Include payment on all loans, including vehicle and equipment purchases on time payment.
- Capital purchases
  - Non-expensed (depreciable) expenditures such as equipment, building purchases on time payment, and leasehold improvements.
- Other start-up costs
  - Expenses incurred prior to first-month projection and paid for after start-up.

- Withdrawals:
  - Should include payment for such things as owner's income tax, social security, health insurance, and executive life insurance premiums.
- Reserves:
  - Insurance, tax, or equipment escrow to reduce the impact of large periodic payments.

Step 4: Total Cash Paid Out

- Add the totals of Steps 2 and 3.

Step 5: Cash Position (End on Month)

- Subtract Step 4 from Step 1.

Key Indicators and Ratios

Being able to summarize your important financial points allows the funders to get an insight into whether or not you understand how the money world operates. The financial industry judges your potential success by international standards and ratios.

If you struggle with numbers ask an accountant to calculate the following ratios:

- Current ratio (1 to 1 or better): current assets divided by current liabilities.
- Quick ratio (0.5 to 1 or better): current assets less inventory divided by current liabilities.
- Debt to worth ratio (3 to 1 or better): creditors capital to owner's capital.
- Gross profit margin (60 percent or better): gross sales less cost of goods sold.
- Net profit margin (10 percent or better): gross sales to net income.

- Debt coverage ratio (1.25 to 1 or better): net income divided by debt payment (principal and interest).
- A/R turnover ratio (as close to 12 as possible): gross sales divided by accounts receivable.

Rainmaker Observation: There are many good computer financial programs available to assist you in formatting your projections. After you have taken a run at the numbers by yourself, it is always a good idea to have your accountant look them over.

CHAPTER 20

Capital Raising Presentation

Funding Steps

There are two steps to funding your concept, project, or company.

- First, you must prepare a persuasive market-driven and investor-centered business plan. A well-documented and targeted plan is 50 percent to getting your loans.
- Second, you must successfully present your plan to investors. Seeking financing requires courage; this endeavor is not for the weak, timid, or impulsive man or woman.

Proposal Evaluation

Whether you are seeking debt or equity financing, start by looking at bank managers, venture capitalists, or private investors as people who adhere to certain financing criteria and policies. And accept that they have set these policies up for specific reasons. One such reason is that they receive hundreds of requests weekly and have limited funds to invest. They are thus in control of the process, and many would see the situation in this manner: *If I lose out on a great project, there will always be another 10 great projects tomorrow.*

Consequently, these funders have a primary goal to quickly eliminate any request that seems to have the slightest flaw. This five-step evaluation process explains funders' methodology:

- Filter out requests according to their sphere of interest.
- Screen out any request that doesn't meet funders' criteria.
- Evaluate those requests that do meet criteria.

- Select the top five requests.
- Request meetings with the selected entrepreneurs.

Filter

The funder first sorts through business plans and quickly rejects proposals that don't fit the established criteria. This rigid criterion defines their investment policy and usually concern the following:

- Your location.
- The industry you are involved in.
- Whether you are targeting a niche market or a general business area.
- The amount of money you require.
- Poorly prepared or template plans.

Ninety percent of the proposals submitted to funders are rejected during the initial sorting phase. Basic templates with blanks to be filled in and other easily recognizable downloadable plans are promptly rejected.

Screen

The plan is next screened for management, feasibility, and product/services. The quality of the CEO, board of directors, and key personnel is a principle screening asset. The investor focuses on key factors such as competence and character issues of your team, capable management, and unquestioned integrity.

Evaluate

The evaluation phase is broad and subjective, and focuses on the market niche, financials, and technology.

The life cycle of the product or service is reviewed and analyzed. You will need a product line that will boost sales over a period of years.

Select

Lastly, funders take their time, though you may have little time. They often monitor an investment project for up to 6 months, and this timeline depends upon investment level, quality of documentation, and the complexity of the proposal.

In the real world, funders use your business plan as an indication of your professionalism and desire to succeed, both in terms of its preparation and presentation. After all, you are asking someone to place large funds in your hands. Keep this evaluation process in mind when preparing your plan.

Funding Stages

There are essentially five stages of project funding requirements. Each stage has specific funding needs.

Seed Capital

Seed capital enables you to pay for the initial evaluation of your business concept. As such, it enables you to pay for market analysis, due diligence, prototype analysis and development, and the preparation of a professional business plan.

Start-Up Capital

Funds are used to purchase fixed and variable assets that enable you to launch your business or product.

Two Rounds of Financing

Funding is required to expand the business into a more established company and then to finance growth into new products and regions. Funds are also used to expand marketing activities and manufacturing capability.

Working Capital Loans

These are funds acquired to gain market share.

Additional Information

It is always a good idea to have the following information ready, in case they are asked for:

- List of fixed assets.
- Updated asset appraisals.
- Personal financial statements.
- Company and personal credit reports.
- Business and personal tax returns.
- Articles of incorporation.
- Copies of orders.
- Customer, bank, and trade references.
- Copies of patents, trademarks, or licenses

Presentation

General Guidelines

Take note of the following:

- First impressions are critical and lasting.
- Use color in the cover of your presentation.
- Bind the material in such a way that allows for easy reading.
- Each section should be easy to find.
- Information must be concise, clear, and logical.
- Use diagrams and tables where possible.
- Support assumptions with research and statistics.

After developing a business plan, consider making visuals an integral part of your presentation to investors. Visuals are a dramatic way to present quantitative information in a condensed, easy-to-read form. Research shows that about half of us are verbally oriented and the other half are visually oriented.

As half of your funders would get their information from the narrative and the other half would get most of their information from visuals, it is necessary to cater to both types of investors.

Proposal visuals can consist of the following:

- Lists
- Tables and charts
- Graphics and maps
- Illustrations and drawings
- Photographs

Visuals must be informative and convincing. The use of these tools will help you to accomplish the following:

- Consolidate and focus critical information
- Depict basic data graphically
- Identify patterns
- Facilitate analysis and evaluation
- Add emphasis
- Improve comprehension and retention

Management Illustrations

These illustrations are used to summarize data and present key points. Such visuals support conclusions in your narrative and are called technical. They usually appear in your exhibits or as attachments to your plan.

The guidelines for management visuals are as follows:

- Keep them simple.
- Make sure that the key point of each visual is clear.
- Integrate visuals with narrative or oral presentation so that they work well together.
- Eliminate immaterial information from your visuals.

Technical Visuals: These visuals let the investors draw their own conclusions. These visuals are usually complex and require special knowledge to understand them completely. Use technical visuals sparingly in your presentation. The guidelines for technical visuals are as follows:

- Review symbols, abbreviations, and other conventions for accuracy and clarity.
- Make sure your visuals are uncluttered.

- Provide data to back up conclusions.
- Use captions to help your investor interpret the data.
- Schedule of assets.
- Personal financial statements.
- Credit report releases.
- Business tax returns.
- Personal tax returns.
- Articles of incorporation.
- Copies of orders or invoices.
- Customer testimonials.
- Trade references.
- Banking references.
- Title reports (equipment, real estate, etc.).
- Asset appraisals.
- Patents, trademarks, or licenses.

In Summary

Research tells us that an effective presentation has to fulfill the following guidelines:

- 8 percent words.
- 36 percent tone of voice.
- 56 percent appearance.
- First impressions are lasting, so make a good one.
- Use a colored product brochure as a cover.
- Bind the material in such a way that allows for easy reading.
- Tab each section for direct access.
- Keep your information concise and to the point.
- Pictures are worth a thousand words, so include good ones.
- Support assumptions with facts, not more assumptions.

Rainmaker Observation: Your goal is to communicate information and emphasize the key points of your plan. So regardless of the specific technique used, make the focus of your visuals clear and easy to understand.

CHAPTER 21

Last Word—Be Wary
of Overtrading

As a precursor remark to this final chapter, be wary that chasing profits can lead to overtrading, which can have similar negative results as undertrading.

How Is the Term Overtrading Defined?

Overtrading is simply the rapid rise in sales without enough cash flow and capital to fund the increased trading. This is risky and a problem because you may run out of working capital and consequently place your company at risk of sequestration. Remember that banks use ratios to measure your risk exposure, and these have been reviewed in this book.

So, how do you know if you are overtrading, and what can you do about it?

As a starting point, overtrading occurs when any of the following occurs:

- There is a rapid rise in sales without a commensurate rise in working capital.
- Management use fixed assets as collateral to raise additional debt or they sell fixed assets to obtain cash.
- Debtors and stock are increased to sustain the growing level of sales.
- The foregoing results in liquidity ratios getting worse to a level of becoming a problem.
- Consequently, ratios can be used to prevent overtrading.

- ○ **Current Ratio** = current assets divided by current liabilities. This is a measure of how much of total current assets are financed by current liabilities. Safe ratios tend to depend on the industry, but a general rule of thumb is that a ratio of 2:1 or greater is considered a safe measure.
- ○ **Quick Ratio** = current assets less inventory and divided by current liabilities. This is a measure of how well current liabilities are covered by liquid assets. A ratio of 1:1 means that you can meet existing liabilities when they are due for payment.
- ○ **Payable days:** Your cash position is getting worse if payable days are getting longer.

Danger Signs of Overtrading

- **Danger sign 1. You need to increase your overdraft to pay variable costs:** If you don't have the cash resources to meet these costs, it could lead to banks and other funders withdrawing loans. This tends to become a multiplier effect. If one bank withdraws a loan, many will follow.
- **Danger sign 2. Profit margins are low:** A substantial rise in sales often results in prices being driven down as competition increases. This will drive down profit margins and add to your worsening cash-flow position. This will occur if you cannot decrease costs of sales.
- **Danger sign 3. Customers and Suppliers.** Without regular payment from customers you may not be able to pay your suppliers, which could be the final straw for your business if you have a cash flow that is already under pressure.

Solution to Overtrading?

- Convert short-term debt to long-term financing, giving you some time relief.
- Finance working capital with short-term finance.

Final Rainmaker Observation: From an economic perspective, it is high-growth companies that are helping reduce unemployment. It would be pointless to see employment turning into retrenchments because you are unable to balance growth with cash-flow management. It is simple. Your bank balance tells it all. If your balance falls, take remedial action. Funders won't ask you to do that.

APPENDIX

By the Same Author

- Share Analysis and Company Forecasting
- The Business Plan: A Manual for South African Entrepreneurs
- The Millionaire Portfolio
- Jungle Tactics: Global Research, Investment and Portfolio Strategies
- A Guide to AltX: Listing on SA's Alternative Stock Exchange
- Become Your Own Stockbroker
- The Corporate Mechanic: The Analytical Strategist's Guide
- Richer Than Buffett: Day Trading to Ultra-Wealth
- The Guerrilla Principle: Winning Tactics for Global Project Managers
- Women and Wealth
- Lore of the Global Trader
- Master Trader
- Business and Entrepreneurship
- The Penny Share Millionaire
- Welcome to My Trading Room: Volume 1: Foundation of Trading
- Welcome to My Trading Room: Volume 2: Create Your Own Brokerage
- Welcome to My Trading Room: Volume 3: Advanced Methodologies and Strategies

General Key Personnel Attributes

Management and Key Staff

The aim of senior management, also called *key management,* is to focus their skills and experience and to effectively use available resources and technological systems to attain profit goals. While management understands that it must provide effective leadership and support to attain profits, the following is a list of attributes.

Positive	Negative
• Develop and implement an appropriate organizational structure • Establish a knowledgeable board of directors • Develop plans to achieve clearly stated measurable objectives • Draft business plans, strategies, policies, and procedures to support the company's objectives • Effect communication systems • Establish effective reporting principles	• Unable to increase market share • Cannot achieve profits • Cannot respond to competitive forces • Indecisiveness • Objectives and strategies are unclear • Lack of coordinated controls, communication, and reporting mechanisms

Marketing and Sales

Marketing objectives are to develop long-term customers and to continually increase this customer base to maximize sales from a loyal base.

Positive	Negative
• Develop effective distribution channels • Market research and analysis is concise and relevant • Promotion and advertising programs are strong and effective • Sales team understands the market • Sales forecasting is accurate	• Lack of market understanding • Lack of coordinated and effective market strategy • Sales incentives are not effective • Sales quotas are continually not met • Poor sales training • High turnover of sales personnel • Low morale • Customer complaints vastly outweigh compliments

Accounting and Finance

Finance's role is to maintain complete financial records and to provides reports to key staff, such as budgets, forecasts, ratio analysis and cost analysis. In addition, finance has the critical responsibility to establish strong internal controls to protect the company against hackers and theft.

Positive	Negative
• Timely financial reporting • Smooth and effective accounting processes • Generation of cash flow analysis, forecasts, accounting, and budgets • Periodic review and control of capital expenditures • Proper asset control measures • Increase in the value of assets • Effective internal auditing of program budgets	• Infrequent financial reporting • Failure to monitor expenditures • Failure to report variances • Lack of documented procedures • Discrepancies • Declining cash management performance • Poor inventory turnover • Inability to identify financial trends • Lack of standards and forecasts • No internal auditing

Human Resources

The objective of HR is to develop and maintain a capable professional, technical, and skilled personnel.

Positive	Negative
• Develop compensation policies and incentives • Ensure that remuneration packages reflect industry norms • Establish harmonious relations with unions • Set up staff performance evaluations • Filing system to hold personnel records • Promote staff training	• Low morale and high personnel turnover • High absenteeism • No respect for management, customers, and clients • Labor strikes and slowdowns • Poor communication • Lack of staff training program

Basic Due Diligence Checklist

General field of investigation
General
Corporate image
Financial statements
Assets
Employees
Sales strategy
Marketing
Industry in which the company operates
Competition
Systems
Legal, corporate, and tax issues
Company contracts and leases
Suppliers

General

- Do you have a business plan?
- General information regarding the company: address, contact details, directors' resumes, etc.
- Origins of the company/history/key achievements/milestones.
- Company facilities.
- The capital required—what is it intended for? Provide a breakdown.
- Business and corporate objectives.
- A brief overview of company changes since inception.
- SWOT analysis.
- Do you have in place an industry/market analysis related to competitors, market trends, and other environmental factors that could affect investor sentiment after an AltX listing? These factors include the following:
  - Political/union
  - Economic
  - Business/finance
  - Technological
- Overview of the industry in which you compete and operate.
- Your competitive edge.
- Do you have a company profile?
- Do you have an Internet site?
- Do you have a marketing/communication strategy?
- Key success factors (value drivers).
- Strategy and implementation.

Corporate Image

- What is the company's public image? Have there been any tensions between the community and the company?
- Has there been anything in the media that would reflect negatively on the company? If so, how has the company dealt with significant negative publicity?
- Are there any pending lawsuits against the company?
- Is the company willing to accept limitations on the publicity?

Financial Statements

- Detailed income statement, cash flow statement, and balance sheet (annual reports) for the past 3 years up to the present moment. Plus forecasts for as many years as you may have.
- All supporting schedules to the foregoing financial statements for the periods listed.
- These schedules should be split by major product lines, if available. There should be separate schedules for local and international markets.
- Accounts receivable per major customer for the past 3 years.
- Physical inventory summary or detailed breakdown of inventory (raw materials, work in process (labor and overhead)) for the past 3 years.
- Accounts payable by vendors for the past 3 years.
- Listing of accrued expenses for the past 3 years.
- Tax returns for the past 3 years.

Marketing

- Customer order reports. This is split up per customers and product lines for a period of at least 3 years.
- Listing of shipments by customers and product lines for the past 3 years up to the present moment.
- Listing of outstanding customer contracts and outstanding customer bids for the domestic, export, and international divisions.
- Description of all manufacturers' representative organizations, agreements, and commission schedules.
- A list of buying sources: domestic, export, and international.
- A list of customers, contracts, and outstanding payments.
- Products, services, sales, and pricing strategies.

Personnel

- Management and shareholder structures, plus group organogram.
- All employment contracts or agreements.

- All bonuses, deferred compensation, share option schemes, profit sharing, and retirement programs.
- All pension plan documentation, including actuarial reports, tax returns, and funding requirements for the past 3 years.
- Schedule of hourly wage rates and number of personnel at each rate.
- Organization chart of salaried personnel.

Contracts and Agreements

- All contracts or agreements with:
  - Vendors and customers
  - Employees
  - Unions
  - Other third parties
- All recent (within 3 years) appraisals of property, machinery, and equipment.
- A list of machinery and equipment. Please provide information on:
  - Assets owned
  - Financed
  - Net asset value (NAV)
  - Values of assets (depreciated and net)
- All outstanding insurance claims.
- All patents, copyrights, and license agreements.
- All lease or purchase agreements for machinery and equipment, vehicles, and property.
- Legal descriptions of all property, including deeds, title reports, and title insurance documentation, together with documentation of any lien thereon.
- Listing and description of all outstanding litigations or anticipated litigations.
- Is union contract transferable? If yes, then description of mechanics of making transfer, such as required approvals.

Ratio Analysis

Ratio analysis equations

Area	Ratios	Calculation of Ratio
Solvency	• General solvency check	[(Fixed assets + investments + current assets) ÷ (long-term loans + current liabilities)] × 100
Liquidity	• Current asset ratio	Current assets ÷ current liabilities
	• Quick ratio (acid test)	(Current assets − stock) ÷ current liabilities
	• Stock-to-working capital ratio	(Stock ÷ net current assets) × 100
	• Defensive interval ratio	Defensive assets ÷ projected daily operating expenses
Profitability	• Profit margins	(Any profit figure ÷ turnover) × 100
	• Return on shareholders' equity	(Attributable profits ÷ shareholders' funds) × 100
	• Return on net assets	(Attributable profits net assets) × 100
	• Return on capital employed	(Operating income capital employed) × 100
Efficiency	• Stock turn	Group turnover average stock
	• Accounts receivable days	Accounts receivable ÷ (turnover ÷ 365)
	• Accounts payable days	Accounts payable ÷ (turnover ÷ 365)
Leverage	• Debt–equity ratio (gearing)	[(long- and short-term loans + overdraft − cash) ÷ Ordinary shareholders' funds] × 100
	• Proportional debt ratio	Long-term loans ÷ total assets
	• Ordinary shareholders' interest	(Ordinary shareholders' funds ÷ loans) × 100
	• Long-term debt to capital employed	(Long-term loans ÷ capital employed) × 100
	• Interest cover	Pretax income ÷ interest paid
	• Average interest rate	(Interest Expense − accounts payable) ÷ liabilities
	• Gross cash flow-to-total debt ratio	[Gross cash flow (prior dividends) ÷ loan] × 100
	• Cash flow-to-assets ratio	Cash from operations ÷ total assets

Area	Ratios	Calculation of Ratio
Investment Performance Ratios	• Earnings per share (EPS)	(Attributable profit ÷ Ordinary Issued Shares) × 100
	• Dividend per share	(Dividends payable ÷ Ordinary Issued Shares) × 100
	• Dividend cover	EPS ÷ dividend per share
	• Earnings yield	(EPS ÷ share price) × 100
	• Dividend yield	(Dividend per share ÷ share price) × 100
	• Dividend payout ratio	Yearly dividend per share ÷ EPS
	• Price–earnings ratio	Inverse of earnings yield
	• Price–earnings growth (PEG)	Price–earnings ratio ÷ company's projected year-over-year earnings growth rate
	• Book value per share	(Shareholders' equity − preferred stock) ÷ average outstanding shares
	• Debt–asset ratio	Total liabilities ÷ total assets

Liquidity: It is the measure of how much free cash there is in the business. This is critically important. The more cash the business has, the less the risk that is attached to the business. It not only cushions the business against bad months from a sales perspective but also allows the business to grow faster and perhaps take advantage of special offers and bulk buying opportunities, which can improve profit margins even further.

Current ratio	> 1 = okay > 2 = preferred
Quick ratio	> 1 = good
Net working capital	> 0 = okay but no room to move > 3× total expenses is good. 6× or 12× is a lot better.

Assets: It is a measure of how well certain assets are being utilized.

• **Debtors' days ratio:** This helps the entrepreneur to understand how quickly the debtors are paying and is a measure of how efficient the organization is at collecting its money.

- **Creditors' days:** This helps the entrepreneur to understand how quickly the creditors are being paid and is a measure of how efficient the business is at collecting its money. It also indicates how much leeway there is in its payment terms.
- **Fixed asset turnover:** This is a measure of how well-fixed assets are being utilized in generating sales.
- **Current asset turnover:** This is a measure of how well current assets are being utilized in generating sales.
- **Total asset turnover:** This is the harshest measure indicating how well total assets are being used in generating sales.

Debt ratios: These ratios measure the gearing of the business, that is, the amount of debt the business has.

- **Debt ratio:** an indicator of how much debt a business has in relation to its assets.
- **Debt equity:** an indicator of how much debt a business has in relation to the equity it has.

| <1 | The business is in deep trouble and is unlikely to be able to continue. |
| >1 | The business is doing well. |

Profitability ratios: These ratios measure the profitability of the business in different ways.

- **Return on equity:** This ratio measures the return on the shareholders' equity. It is a measure of how efficient the business is in using the equity to generate profit.
- **Return on total assets:** This ratio measures the return on the business's assets. It is a measure of how efficient the business is at using the assets to generate profit.

Glossary

Acceleration clause. Clause requiring repayment of a debt if specified events occur or specific terms are not met.

Acceptance criteria. The criteria by which a product or system is judged at acceptance testing. Usually derived from commercial or other requirements.

Acceptance date. Time limit given to a prospective shareholder to accept an offer of shares in a "rights" issue.

Acceptance test. The final functional testing used to evaluate the state of a product and determine its readiness for the end user. A "gateway" or "milestone" that must be passed.

Account. A trading period whose dates are fixed by the stock exchange authorities.

Accountability. To ensure that a result is achieved, usually through the effort of others.

Accounting policies. Principles, bases, conventions, rules, and procedures adopted by management in preparing and presenting financial statements.

Accounts payable. Bills which have to be paid as part of the normal course of business.

Accounts receivable. Debts owed to your company from credit sales.

Accumulated depreciation. Total accumulated depreciation reduces the book value (formal accounting value) of assets. The value of an asset is reduced each month by a predetermined amount and timeframe. An asset worth $100, depreciated by $10 per month, would be written off over 10 months.

Accuracy rating. A high, medium, or low rating that depicts the level of confidence that the team has in an estimate.

Acid test. A ratio used to determine how liquid a company is. It is determined by subtracting short-term assets from accounts receivable and inventory which is then divided by short-term liabilities.

Ad hoc. Member attendance at team meetings is by invitation only.

Affinity diagram. A team-based tool for identifying and organizing ideas.

Agenda. Notice of a meeting that states meeting location, time, and date of the meeting and the items to be discussed.

Agent. A member who acts on behalf of a client and has no personal interest in the order.

AIM. The anagram for the UK-based Alternative Investment Market.

Alpha. It is the first version of product where all of the intended functionality has been implemented, but interface has not been completed, and bugs have not been fixed.

Analyze. The first phase in many developmental and delivery methodologies. The analyze phase involves examination of the proposal to determine the requirements and "what" is to be addressed by the project.

Arbitrage. A purchase or sale by a member on his or her own account of securities on one stock exchange with the intent to sell or buy those securities on another stock exchange to profit by the difference between the prices of those securities on such stock exchanges.

Asset swap. A transaction that complies with all the requirements of their Federal Banks in respect of the same.

Asset turnover. Sales divided by total assets. Important for comparison over time and to other companies of the same industry.

Assumptions. Statements describing situations that are taken to be true.

Authorized/issued share capital. While the authorized share capital is the maximum number of shares a company is permitted to issue over time, the issued share capital is the actual number of shares in issue. These figures are specified in preincorporation agreements (memorandum and articles of association). Investors can find these figures in a company's annual report.

Bad debts. An amount payable by debtors that the firm determines is irrecoverable.

Balance sheet. A statement that shows a company's financial position on a particular date.

Bankers' acceptance. A bill of exchange, or draft, drawn by the borrower for payment on a specified date and accepted by a chartered bank. Upon acceptance, the bill becomes, in effect, a postdated certified cheque.

Bankruptcy. A legal procedure for formally liquidating a business carried out under the jurisdiction of courts of law.

Baseline. A snapshot at a point in time of part of a project plan. A "schedule baseline" is a snapshot of the schedule at that point in time which can be compared over time.

Benefits realization review. The process of reviewing the extent of realized benefits once the solution has been delivered and implemented. Measured benefits are compared with those originally proposed in the business case.

Benefits tracking. The process of quantitatively measuring over a period of time the extent of realized benefits once the solution has been delivered and implemented.

Best efforts. This term is used to describe a deal in which underwriters only agree to "do their best" in selling shares to the public. An initial public offering (IPO) is more commonly provided on a bought-or-firm commitment basis in which the underwriters are obligated to sell the allotted shares.

Beta. It is the first version of a product where all of the functionality has been implemented and the interface is complete, but the product still has problems or defects.

Blank check. A company that indicates no specific industry, business, or venture when its securities are publicly offered for sale and the proceeds of the offering are not specifically allocated.

Bond. Usually a fixed-interest security under which the issuer contracts to pay the lender a fixed principal amount at a stated date in the future and a series of interest payments, either semiannually or annually. Interest payments may vary throughout the life of the bond.

Book value. The net amount of an asset shown in the books of a company, that is, the cost of purchasing a fixed asset less the depreciation on that asset.

Bookkeeping. The process of collecting, classifying, recording, and summarizing a business financial transactions in what are known as journals and ledgers.

Bottom Up. Building or designing a product from elementary building blocks, starting with the smaller elements and evolving into a larger structure.

Brainstorming. A technique for generating ideas.

Break-even point. The unit sales volume or actual sales amount that a company needs to equal its running expenses rate and not lose or make money in a given month. Breakeven is based on regular running expenses, unlike the standard accounting formula that is based on technical fixed expenses.

Broker. The name given to a natural person recognized by an official stock exchange.

Budget risk. The risk of potential problems that could cause the team to overspend the budget.

Budget. Planned expenditure and funds allocated for a project.

Burden rate. Refers to personnel burden, which is the sum of employer costs above salaries.

Business process. A set of steps that turns inputs into repetitive outputs. One of the ways, besides projects, by which work is accomplished.

Business case. A document detailing the justification for the proposed business project.

Business owner. The person(s) in the organization that will take ownership of the project's outputs and use them for the benefit of the organization.

Business requirements specification. A document that states specifically the business needs that the project's outputs must satisfy. It is basically the "what" aspect of the project.

CAPEX. Capital expenditure. Typically includes purchase of new equipment.

Capital assets. Long-term assets, also known as fixed assets (plant and equipment).

Capital expenditure. Expenses made on capital assets.

Capital input. New money being invested in the business. New capital will increase your cash and will also increase the total amount of paid-in capital.

Capital structure. Usually refers to the structure of ordinary and preference shares and long-term liabilities.

Capital turnover. Annual sales divided by average stockholder equity (net worth) (i.e., total sales for each dollar of equity).

Capital. This is also known as total shares in issue, owner's equity, or shareholders' funds.

Capitalization. The total amount of debt and equity issued by a company.

Cash Budget. A plan or projection of cash receipts and disbursements for a given period of time. It is essential for the determination of cash deficiencies or excess cash balances.

Cash conversion cycle. The time it takes for a company to pay cash for a product, add its value to the product, and then receive cash from the sale of that product.

Cash equivalents. Instruments or investments of such high liquidity and safety that they are virtually equal to cash.

Cash flow. A statement that shows the net difference between cash received and paid during the company's operating cycle.

Cash. The bank balance, or checking account balance, or real cash in bills and coins.

Cash-flow forecast. An estimate of the timing and amount of a company's inflow and outflow of money measured over a specific period of time; typically, monthly for 1 to 2 years, then annually for an additional 1 to 3 years.

Change log. The means by which a project leader tracks the status of change requests.

Change management. A structured process for making changes to the project plan.

Change request. A request from inside or outside the project to amend the project plan.

Change control. The set of practices around effectively managing changes to the project so that they are raised, assessed, prioritized, and implemented efficiently and with a known impact on the project.

Charter. A document stating the desired output of the initiation phase. It outlines the expectations and constraints that the team has when they plan the project.

Close-out stage. The final project management phase in which the project is evaluated, feedback is elicited, and lessons learned are captured.

Close-out report. The output of the close-out phase. It includes the final status report, evaluation and feedback documents, lessons learned, and recommendations for improving the project system.

Collection period (days). The average number of days that pass between delivering an invoice and receiving the money.

Collections days. See Collection period

Commission. The brokers charge a fee for buying and selling shares, which is brokerage or commission earned on a deal.

Commissions percent. An assumed percentage used to calculate commissions expense as the product of this percentage multiplied by gross margin.

Conceptual view. A very high-level summary of what the solution will look like once it is implemented. It can be presented as a diagram.

Consensus. Agreement within a group to a decision that everyone can live with.

Constraint. Something that the team is not allowed to do or a resource that is not available to the project.

Contingency. Reserve resources (time, effort, or money) that are set aside because of the unpredictability of the future.

Convertible and redeemable preference shares. An alternative mechanism to ordinary shares. It enables companies to issue other shares that can either be bought back from investors or converted into ordinary shares at a later date.

Corporate finance transaction. A transaction that is entered into in writing and requires public notification in the press in terms of the listings requirements of an exchange.

Cost of sales. The costs associated with producing the sales. In a standard manufacturing or distribution company, this is about the same as the costs for people delivering the service or subcontracting costs.

Cost risk. The same as budget risk. The risk of potential problems that could cause the team to overspend the budget.

Countermeasure. An activity or deliverable that will prevent or reduce a risk.

Credit risk. Risk that a borrower may default on obligations, thus posing a danger that repayment will not take place.

Creditors. People or companies that you owe money to. This is the old name for accounts payable.

Criteria. The factors used to make a decision.

Critical path. The minimum set of tasks that must be completed to conclude a phase or a project. The path through the schedule in which there is no slack. The critical path is the longest path through the schedule, and it determines the final delivery date in the project.

Crossed market. Where a bid price is higher than the offer price for a security.

Current assets. Those assets that can be quickly converted into cash and include accounts receivable, stock, and debtors book. These are often called liquid assets.

Current debt. Short-term debt or short-term liabilities.

Current liabilities. A company's short-term debt, which must be paid within the firm's operating cycle, that is, less than 1 year.

Customer acceptance criteria. The criteria the customer will use to determine if he or she is satisfied with the final deliverable.

Customer evaluation. An assessment by the customer, after the final deliverable has been delivered, of his or her level of satisfaction with the project.

Customer need. The problem that the final deliverable will help the customer resolve.

Customer requirements. Specific features or functions that the customer wants from the final deliverable.

Deadline. The date for delivery of a deliverable that is set by someone outside the project team, usually the sponsor or customer.

Deal breaker. A significant issue relating to the proposed financing between the prospective investor and the entrepreneur that must be resolved in order to close the deal.

Debenture. A bond that is not secured by fixed assets.

Debt and equity. The sum of liabilities and capital. This should always be equal to total assets.

Debtors. People or companies that owe your company money. It is the old name for accounts receivable.

Decision options. The choices available before a final decision is made.

Deliverable. An item produced by a project or part of a project that is tangible and objectively verifiable.

Deliverables schedule. The schedule that shows the delivery date for each of the project's deliverables and the interdependencies between them.

Deliverables staff effort. The internal effort required to create the deliverables for the project.

Delivery date. The date a deliverable is scheduled to be turned over to the next customer in the technical process.

Demand loan. A loan that must be repaid in full on demand.

Depreciated replacement value. The value of an asset with reference to the cost of replacing the asset with a new asset of similar utility minus an amount reflecting the depreciation of the existing asset.

Depreciation. An accounting and tax concept used to estimate the loss of value of assets over time. For example, cars depreciate with use.

Dilution. A reduction in per share participation in net earnings and ownership through an increase in the issued stock.

Directive project management. The old management approach in which the project manager did the planning, delegated tasks to team members, monitored the project, and then shut it down.

Discount rate. A rate of return used to convert a monetary sum, payable or receivable in the future, into present value.

Discounted cash flow (DCF). Techniques for establishing the relative worth of a future investment by discounting (at a required rate of return) the expected net cash flow from the project.

Discounting. The process of finding the present value of a series of future cash flows. It is the reverse of compounding.

Divestiture. The sale of part of a company. It is the opposite of a merger.

Dividend coverage. Number of times a company's dividend is covered by earnings available to pay it.

Due diligence review. The investigatory and review procedures carried out by strategists, accountants, and lawyers.

Due diligence. A reasonable investigation conducted by the parties involved in preparing a disclosure document to form a basis for believing that the statements contained therein are true and that no material facts are omitted.

Duration. The length of calendar time required to complete a project or part of a project.

Earned value analysis. A technique for determining the value delivered by a project to date compared with what it planned to deliver in the first place.

Earnings. Also called income or profits, earnings are the famous "bottom line": sales less costs of sales and expenses.

Earnout. A method of structuring a transaction whereby the ultimate purchase price depends in part on the future performance of the business being acquired.

EBIT. Earnings before interest and taxes.

EBITDA. Earnings before interest, income taxes, depreciation, and amortization.

Effort. The measure of the amount of work required to complete a project or part of a project.

Empirical approach. A valuation approach whereby the value of a company is determined by reference to open-market transactions involving similar companies or by reference to value relationships implied in the stock price of publicly traded companies.

End customer. The customer that will ultimately use the product or service being developed. The end user.

End user. The person who uses a product, service, or process.

End-user requirements. The performance characteristics of the final product, service, or process that are requested by the end user.

Equity. Business ownership; capital. Equity can be calculated as the difference between assets and liabilities.

Escrow. An agreement put into the custody of another party until certain conditions are fulfilled.

Estimate. A calculated guess of the size, cost, and duration of a future project.

Evaluate. A phase in some project methodologies in which the success of the project in meeting its objectives is measured and reported.

Exchange risk. The risk associated with an asset or liability denominated in a foreign currency. It is vulnerable to the movement of exchange rates.

Execution stage. The stage in the project management process in which the deliverables are created and their progress is tracked.

Executive summary. A concise summary of an investment proposal that describes a company's background, products or services, financial needs, financial requirements, management capabilities, market description, and financial data.

Exit options. A variety of options available to investors to recover their invested capital and the return on their investment.

Expectations. It is what the client hopes will be accomplished.

Expected return. The total amount of money (return) an investor anticipates to receive from an investment.

External costs. Expenses for the project that originate outside the organization.

External customer. A customer who resides outside the organization.

Facilitation. The act of helping a person or group to work through a process.

Feature/scope creep. The relentless tendency of a project to self-inflate and take on more features or functionality than what was originally intended. Also known as "scope creep."

Features. Specific attributes of final deliverables.

Final deliverable. The final output from the execution stage of the project that is delivered to the project customer.

Final status report. The last status report for the project that is completed after the project client has accepted the final deliverable.

Financial notes. Information explaining financial figures (balance sheet, income statement, and cash flow).

Fixed costs. Running costs that take time to wind down: usually rent, overhead, and some salaries. Technically, fixed costs are those that the business would continue to pay even if it went bankrupt. In practice, fixed costs are usually considered the running costs.

Fiscal year. Standard accounting practice allows the accounting year to begin in any month. Fiscal years are numbered according to the year in which they end. For example, a fiscal year ending in February of 1992 is fiscal year 1992, even though most of the year takes place in 1991.

Fixed assets. Includes all fixed (immovable) assets, namely property, vehicles, machinery, and equipment. It cannot usually be converted into cash within the firm's operating cycle.

Fixed expenses. Cost of doing business that does not change with the volume of business. Examples might be rent for business premises, insurance payments, and heat and light.

Fixed rate loan. Loan for a fixed period of time with a fixed interest rate for the life of the loan.

Flipping. This is when an investor has acquired an IPO at its offering price and sells it immediately for a quick gain soon after it starts trading on the open market. A practice discouraged by underwriters that can lead such investors to unfavorable relationships with their underwriters with future IPOs.

Floating charge. Charge or assignment on a company's total assets as security for a loan on total assets without citing specific assets.

Floating rate. A situation where the interest rate or rate of exchange is determined solely by market forces.

Forecast. Future-oriented financial information prepared using assumptions, all of which reflect the entity's planned courses of action for the period covered, given management's judgment as to the most probable set of economic conditions.

Foreign exchange. Claims payable abroad in a foreign currency, including bank deposits, bills, and checks. Foreign exchange rates refer to the number of units of one currency required to buy another.

Forming stage. The first stage of team development. It is when people are getting to know one another.

Front-end fees. Fees paid when, for example, a financial instrument such as a loan is arranged.

Front-end loading. Charges or fees that are greater at the starting phase of a loan or investment than in its later stages.

Functional manager. The person accountable for a department or a set of resources. Also known as a resource manager.

Funding consolidation. The process of replacing short-term debt with long-term securities (shares or bonds).

Funding costs. The price of obtaining capital, either borrowed or equity, with intent to carry on business operations.

Gantt chart. A schedule that visually shows the duration for each deliverable or activity.

Going concern. A company that is operating, that is, has not stopped producing goods or providing a service, and one which has not been placed under liquidation or curatorship.

Goodwill. An intangible asset reflected in balance sheets, which indicate an excess over market value for assets paid by the firm.

Gross geographic product. A statistic that shows the remuneration received by the production factors (land, labor, capital, and entrepreneurship) for their participation in production of goods and services in a defined area.

Gross margin percent. Gross margin divided by sales, displayed as a percentage. Acceptable levels depend on the nature of the business.

Gross margin. Sales less cost of sales.

Historical data. Data collected from past projects.

Horizontal analysis. The process of comparing consecutive financial statements by examining the increases or decreases between the periods in terms of absolute dollar and percentages.

Hurdle rate. A predetermined benchmark rate of return. If the rate of return expected from the project or investment falls below the benchmark, the projected investment will no longer be accepted. The hurdle rate should be the marginal cost of capital adjusted for the project's risk.

Hypothecation. The pledge of property and assets to secure a loan. Hypothecation does not transfer title, but it does provide the right to sell the hypothecated property in the event of default.

Immediate deal. A transaction in a listed security where settlement is to take place the next business day.

Impact analysis. The assessment of what effect something will have on the project plan.

Implement. The phase of a project involved with delivering the solution to the business owner.

Income statement. A statement showing net income or loss for a specified period.

Incremental development. The development of a product in a piece-by-piece fashion, allowing for a gradual implementation of functionality without having the whole thing finished.

Initial team. The team originally selected to be on the project.

Initiation. The first project management phase. In this phase the overall direction and constraints for the project are set.

Input–output chain. The workflow of interconnected or interdependent deliverables that creates the final deliverable.

Input. A supply that is used in a process.

Interdependencies. The dependencies that exist in any system, where one team member depends on another for certain inputs or to receive certain outputs.

Interest expense. Interest that is paid on debts and is deducted from profit as expenses.

Interim deliverable. A deliverable that is produced in the technical process before the production of the final deliverable.

Internal costs. Expenses for the project that are cross-charged by a department inside the organization.

Internal customer. A customer that is inside the organization.

Interrelationship digraph. A team-based tool that helps a team identify root causes.

Inventory turnover. Sales divided by inventory. Usually calculated using the average inventory over an accounting period, not an ending-inventory value.

Inventory turns. Inventory turnover (above).

Inventory. This is another name for stock. Goods in stock, either finished goods or materials to be used to manufacture goods.

Issues list. A list to record issues that must be resolved or action items that are not significant enough to be put on the project schedule.

Issues management. A set of practices designed to effectively identify, prioritize, and monitor issues and manage them through to resolution.

Kick-off. Typically, the first meeting of the project team, when the project is officially launched.

Labor. In business plans the word "labor" often refers to the labor costs associated with making goods to be sold. This labor is part of the cost of sales and part of the manufacturing and assembly. In economic terms, labor often denotes the sale of a skill to produce a product or service.

Large project. A project with more than 10 team members.

Letter of acceptance. The investor may receive such a letter if the company accepts his or her application for shares.

Leverage ratio. A financial ratio that measures a firm's debt burden. The debt, times interest earned, and fixed charges coverage ratios are leverage ratios.

Leverage. The relationship between interest-bearing debt and equity in a company (financial leverage) or the effect of fixed expense on after-tax earnings (operating leverage).

Liabilities. Debts; money that must be paid. Usually, debt on terms of less than five years is called short-term liabilities, whereas debt on terms of longer than five years is called long-term liabilities.

Liaison. A person on the project team assigned to communicate with a stakeholder.

Limit order. An order that may only be effected at prices equal to or better than the price on the order.

Liquidity. A company's ability to pay short-term debt with short-term assets.

Listing. The official granting of a listing of a company's shares on a stock exchange.

Long-term assets. Assets like plant and equipment that are depreciated over terms of more than five years and are likely to last that long too.

Long-term interest rate. The interest rate charged on long-term debt. This is usually higher than the rate on short-term debt.

Long-term liabilities. This is the same as long-term loans. Most companies call a debt long term when it is on terms of five years or more.

Management leveraged buyout. The situation when the management of a company purchases all the company's shares or assets. Usually, the company's assets become security for the loans necessary to make the purchase.

Management of investments. The management of investments on behalf of a client by a member or an approved person.

Management. Individuals in an entity that have the authority and the responsibility to manage the entity. The positions of these individuals, and their titles, vary from one entity to another and, to some extent, from one country to another depending on the local laws and customs. Thus, when the context requires it, the term includes the board of directors or committees of the board that are designated to oversee certain matters (e.g., an audit committee).

Market capitalization. Used to denote a company's size and is calculated by multiplying a company's issued share capital by its current share price.

Market indicators. Statistics that give an overall picture of how the market is performing.

Market risk. The part of a security's risk that cannot be eliminated by diversification.

Marketable securities. All instruments legally permitted to trade on a stock exchange. These include shares (ordinary and preference), bonds, futures, and options.

Materials. Included in the cost of sales. These are not just any materials but materials involved in the assembly or manufactured of goods for sale.

Maturity date. The date on which a debt is due for payment.

Mentor. A close personal contact, usually in your industry, who has a network of contacts in the investment community and can assist you in achieving your objectives.

Method. A system for getting something done.

Mezzanine debt. Nonconventional debt that has a greater element of risk than secured debt but less risk than equity.

Milestone schedule. The schedule used to communicate the dates that major accomplishments in the project will be completed.

Milestone. A major accomplishment of a project. A significant point in a project schedule that denotes the delivery of a significant portion of the project. Normally associated with a particular "deliverable."

Minority shareholders. Shareholders who by virtue of their percentage ownership of the company do not have voting control of the company.

Minutes. Notes taken during a meeting that summarize discussions and agreed-on actions.

Monopoly. When one company controls and dominates a particular company.

Mortgage. Debt instrument by which the borrower (mortgagor) gives the lender (mortgagee) a lien on a property as security for the repayment of a loan.

Mourning stage. The last stage in the team-development process.

Multivoting. A team-based tool for selecting one or more options for a decision.

Negative covenant. A promise not to do certain things.

Net cash flow. This is the projected change in cash position, an increase or decrease in cash balance.

Net income. The level of profit in a business after the deduction of income taxes, depreciation, operating expenses, and other expenses. It is also known as after-tax profit or net profit.

Net present value (NPV). A method of ranking investment proposals. NPV is equal to the present value of future returns, discounted at the cost of capital, minus the present value of the cost of the investment.

Net profit. The operating income less taxes and interest. The same as earnings or net income.

Net realizable value. Selling price of an asset minus the expenses of bringing the asset into a saleable state and expenses of the sale.

Net working capital. Total of all current assets minus the total of all current liabilities of a company.

Net worth. This is the same as assets minus liabilities and the same as total equity.

Networking. Making use of contacts, associates, and friends.

Non-assignable. Restriction in a contract limiting the ability of a shareholder to transfer the rights, benefits, or obligations pursuant to that contract.

Non-compete. Generally refers to a clause in a contract that restricts a person from starting a similar business or working for a competitor. It is normally time and area specific.

Oligopoly. A situation when a few companies control and dominate a particular market.

Ordinary shares. A commercial paper issued to investors to raise capital. Investors hold these shares as part owners in the firm.

Other short-term assets. These are securities and business equipment.

Other ST liabilities. These are short-term debts that don't cause interest expenses. For example, they might be loans from founders or accrued taxes (taxes owed, already incurred, but not yet paid)

Output. A product that is produced as a result of a process.

Overheads. Running expenses not directly associated with specific goods or services sold but with the general running of the business

Oversight. The act of high-level monitoring to assure that a project is on track.

Over-the-counter (OTC) market. A market made up of dealers who make a market for those securities not listed on an exchange. An over-the-counter market exists between buyers and sellers over the telephone rather than the electronic market found on some exchanges.

Paid-in capital. Real money paid into the company as investments. This is not to be confused with par value of stock or market value of stock. This is actual money paid into the company as equity investments by owners.

Paper profit. A surplus income over expense, which has not yet been released, that is, share prices that have increased above the price at which they were bought but not yet sold.

Par value. The nominal value of a share and is an arbitrary amount placed on the share by the company.

Participative project management. A new approach to managing a project in which the team collaborates with the project leader to create a project plan, monitor and track the project, and close down the project.

Payment days. The average number of days that pass between receiving an invoice and paying it.

Payroll burden. Payroll burden includes payroll taxes and benefits. It is calculated using a percentage assumption that is applied to payroll. For example, if payroll is $1,000 and the burden rate 10 percent, then the burden is an extra $100. Acceptable payroll burden rates vary by market, by industry, and by company.

Phase gate. A go-no go decision point at the end of each project management stage.

Phase. A set of activities within the project management process.

Plan. A document that describes how something should be accomplished.

Planning stage. The second stage of the project management process in which a plan for how the project will be executed is developed and approved.

Plant and equipment. This is the same as long-term assets, or fixed assets, or capital assets.

Portfolio. A schedule, normally computer generated, listing the relevant details in respect of the securities held by an investor.

Post-implementation review. A review conducted sometime after the completion of a project in order to determine whether the project has met its objectives; usually abbreviated to PIR.

Predecessor. A deliverable or activity that must be done before the next deliverable or activity can be completed.

Price–earnings (P/E) ratio. The market price of securities divided by its earnings. It expresses the number of years' earnings (at the current rate) which a buyer is prepared to pay for a security.

Principal transaction. A transaction where a member trades with a counterparty or another member.

Private placement. An offering of a limited amount of shares or units, in which the recipients receive restricted stock from the issuer.

Process. A set of steps that transforms an input(s) into an output(s).

Product development. Expenses incurred in the development of new products; salaries, laboratory equipment, test equipment, prototypes, research and development, etc.

Product development life cycle. A methodical approach to designing and delivering new products.

Product. A tangible or intangible good produced via a process.

Profit before interest and taxes. This is also known as EBIT, for earnings before interest and taxes. It is gross margin minus operating expenses.

Project management staff effort. The amount of time that people on the project team will spend in project management activities such as attending meetings, writing reports, and planning.

Project management. The application of knowledge, skills, tools, and techniques to meet or exceed customer expectations from a project.

Project objectives. The purpose of a project. The significant accomplishments that the project must achieve.

Project plan. A complete plan for how a project will be executed. The output of the planning phase.

Project priorities. The ranking of the triple constraints for the project—scope versus schedule versus budget.

Project team members. The people on the main project team.

Project board. A group of people ultimately responsible for a project's success through monitoring its progress, reviewing its continued relevance to the organization's objectives, and overcoming institutional barriers. In some organizations, it may be referred to as a steering committee.

Project definition. A document describing succinctly the project objectives, scope, summarized costs, and resource requirements. In some organizations, it may be referred to as the project brief or terms of reference.

Project manager. The person selected by the organization to manage the project resources and activities in order to deliver the agreed-on project outputs.

Project sponsor. A senior person within an organization that has ultimate responsibility for the success of a project through overcoming organizational barriers and advocating for the project. They may devote resources to the project and in some cases is the business owner.

Project. A set of interrelated activities managed in a coordinated way and designed to deliver a unique product or service within a given timeframe and resources.

Projection. Future-oriented financial information prepared using assumptions that reflect the entity's planned courses of action for the period.

Prospectus. This document is an integral part of a documentation that must be filed with the stock exchange. It defines, among many things, the company's type of business, use of proceeds, competitive landscape, financial information, risk factors, and strategy for future growth and also lists its directors and executive officers.

Prototype. A simple model of a product that is used to resolve a design decision in the project.

Published financial. Financial statements and financial information that are made public.

Purchase agreement. A legal document recording the final understanding of the parties with respect to the proposed transaction.

Ratchet clause. A clause in a contract that adjusts the rights of the parties to the contract on the completion of mutually agreed-upon performance criteria.

Rate of return. Return on invested capital (calculated as a percentage). Often, an investor has, as one investment criterion, a minimum acceptable rate of return on an acquisition.

Real property. Real estate, including land and buildings.

Receivable turnover. Sales on credit for an accounting period divided by the average accounts receivable balance.

Recourse. The right to receive payment in the event a person defaults on a loan. Recourse could give the lender the ability to take possession of the borrower's assets.

Redundant assets. Assets that are not required for the ongoing operation of the business and could be withdrawn without affecting future earning potential.

Registration. A new shareholder is registered when his name is placed on the roll of shareholders for a specific company.

Renunciation date. The date set by a company by which a shareholder has to decide whether he or she will take up the rights issue.

Replacement Value. Cost of acquiring a new asset to replace an existing asset with the same functional utility.

Representations. Statements made by either party with respect to certain elements of the proposed transaction that, if proven untrue, may give the other party the right to claim for damages from the party making the warranty.

Requirement. A statement of need from a project stakeholder that identifies a required attribute of the system or product to be delivered.

Research and development incentives. Government programs to promote research and development.

Residual value. Typically estimated based on the present value of the after-tax cash flow expected to be earned after the forecast period.

Resistance. When stocks go up, they tend to reach a point where investors think that they are overvalued, and sellers of the stock outnumber buyers. This causes the price of the stock to stop dead in its tracks. It cannot go higher because there are no buyers. This point is called "resistance."

Resource managers. Also known as functional managers. They provide the resources, primarily the people, to work on the project.

Resource planning. The plan for who will be involved in the project, how much time it will take, and what it will cost.

Resource. People, materials, tools, and systems needed during a project.

Restricted liquidity. Inability of an individual or company to convert an asset into cash, or cash equivalent, without significant cost.

Retained earnings. A figure that shows the sum of a company's net profit less dividends paid to shareholders.

Return on assets. Net profit divided by total assets. A measure of profitability.

Return on equity. A ratio used to show how profitable a business is to the shareholders.

Return on investment. Net profits divided by net worth or total equity; yet another measure of profitability. Also called ROI.

Return on sales. Net profits divided by sales, another measure of profitability.

Return on investment. The financial benefit resulting from a project once the cost of the project is deducted from the financial gain.

Rework. Doing the work over because the work was not done right the first time.

Rights issues. There are several methods that a company can use to increase the size of its share capital. If it decides to offer its existing shareholders first option on the issue, it is called a "rights" issue. The dealers would note that such an issue is in progress as it would be quoted as cum-capitalization and after the completion of the issue it would be quoted as ex-capitalization.

Risk assessment. The process of identifying, analyzing, and preventing risks from occurring.

Risk identification. The process of brainstorming what potential problems might occur in the project.

Risk impact. The effect a risk would have on the project if it occurred.

Risk probability. The likelihood that a risk will occur.

Risk rating. The level of risk that the team determines is in the project.

Risk management. A set of practices designed to effectively identify, prioritize, and monitor risks and plan for their mitigation.

Risk. An event that could possibly occur and which would have an impact on the project if it happens.

ROI (return on investment). A ratio that compares the monetary outlay for a project to the monetary benefit. Used to show the success of a project.

ROI. Return on investment; net profits divided by net worth or total equity; yet another measure of profitability.

Sales breakeven. The sales volume at which costs are exactly equal to sales.

Sales on credit. Sales on credit are sales made on account, shipments against invoices to be paid later.

Schedule risk. Potential problems that could occur that would prevent the team from meeting its deadline dates.

Schedule. The dates of completion for deliverables or activities mapped against the project's timelines.

Scope boundaries. The fence that is placed around the scope of the project to delineate what is inside and outside the project scope.

Scope description. A written explanation of features and functions of the final deliverable.

Scope plan. The part of the project plan that relates to scope. It includes the scope description of the final deliverable, customer acceptance criteria, scope boundaries, and a stakeholder list.

Scope risk. Potential problems that could prevent the team from meeting the customer's acceptance criteria.

Scope. A clear description of the breadth of a project—what is in and what is out.

Scrap value. An amount left after an asset has been fully depreciated, that is, if an asset of $115 is depreciated by $10 per month over 11 months, the scrap value would be $5.

Securities. Includes stocks, shares, debentures (issued by a company having a share capital), notes, units of stock issued in place of shares, options on stocks or shares or on such debentures, notes or units, and rights thereto, and options on indices of information as issued by a stock exchange on prices of any of the aforementioned instruments.

Seed financing/capital. Generally refers to the first contribution of capital toward the financing requirements of a start-up business.

Sensitivity analysis. A technique used to determine the effects on net income or cash flow due to changes in assumptions (i.e., "what if" analysis).

Service. The act of one person doing for another.

Settlement value. Dollar amount of the final payment in a lease.

Settlement. Procedure for brokers to close off their books on a particular transaction. The client is expected to pay for his or her new shares on or before the settlement date, and he or she, in turn, can expect to be paid (on selling shares) within the same period (also called the settlement period).

Share capital. Total shares authorized to be issued, or actually issued, by a company.

Shareholders. Owners of one or more shares in a company.

Short-term assets. Cash, securities, bank accounts, accounts receivable, inventory, business equipment, and assets that last less than five years or are depreciated over terms of less than five years.

Short-term notes. This is the same as short-term loans. These are debts on terms of five years or less.

Short-term. Normally used to distinguish between short-term and long-term, when referring to assets or liabilities. Definitions vary because different companies and accountants handle this in different ways. Accounts payable is always short-term assets. Most companies call any debt of less than five-year terms short-term debt. Assets that depreciate over more than five years (e.g., plant and equipment) are usually long-term assets.

Shotgun. A clause in a shareholder's agreement whereby if one party offers to buy out the other at a certain price, the other party has, within a limited period, the right either to accept the price or buy the offeror out at the same price.

Sinking funds. A required annual payment designed to amortize a bond or an issue of preferred shares. The sinking fund may be held in the form of cash or marketable securities, but generally the money put into the fund is used to retire some of the securities in question each year.

Sizing. A preliminary guess with a wider degree of tolerance than an estimate. The tolerance could be as wide as $\pm$ 50%.

Slack time. Free time that exists between the completion of a predecessor and the start of a successor.

Small project. A project with 10 or fewer team members.

Spending budget. The approved spending estimate.

Spending estimate. The projected costs of the project.

Spending limit. The maximum amount of money that can be spent on the project.

Sponsor evaluation. The evaluation of the project by the sponsor.

Sponsor. The person who acts as a liaison between the project leader and the management team, providing oversight to the project.

Spread. The differential between a bid and an offer price.

Staff effort. The amount of time that people inside the organization will spend on the project.

Staff-effort budget. The approved staff-effort estimate.

Staff-effort costs. The commercial rate for each person or subproject multiplied by the staff-effort estimate for that person or subproject.

Staff-effort estimate. The projected amount of time that each person or subproject will need to spend to complete the project.

Staff-effort limit. The maximum amount of time that people inside the organization can spend working on the project.

Stage gates. Go-no go decision points within the technical process for a project.

Stakeholder group. Stakeholders that have similar interests in a project.

Stakeholder. Any person that may have an interest in the process, outputs, or outcomes of a project.

Standby fee. A fee charged on the unused portion of the credit under a revolving credit or line of credit arrangement.

Starting year. A term to denote the year that a company started operations.

Statement of changes in financial position. A financial document that presents the increases or decreases in funds of a business for all its accounts broken down under three major headings: operating activities, financing activities, and investing activities.

Statement of retained earnings. A financial document that shows how much of the net income of a business has been retained over a given period of time and how much has been paid out to the owners.

Status report. The report issued during the execution phase of the project that denotes whether the project is on track or not.

Steering committee. A group of people ultimately responsible for a project's success through monitoring its progress, reviewing its continued relevance to the organization's objectives, and overcoming institutional barriers. In some organizations, it may be referred to as a project board.

Subordinated debt. A nonconventional financing instrument where the lender accepts a reduced rate of interest in exchange for equity participation.

Subproject leader. The person who leads the subproject team through the project management process.

Subproject team. The group of people who complete the work of a subproject.

Subproject tree. The organizational chart for the project that shows subprojects, deliverables within each subproject, and accountability for each subproject.

Subproject. A subsection of the main project responsible for producing a set of deliverables.

Successor. A deliverable that comes immediately after a predecessor deliverable.

Sustainable growth rate. The rate of increase in sales that a company can attain without changing its profit margin, assets-to-sales ratios, debt-to-equity ratio, or dividend payout ratio. It is the rate of growth that a company can finance without excessive borrowing or a new stock issue.

Syndication. A method of selling an investment through the use of a group of companies or investors.

Tax rate percent. An assumed percentage applied against pretax income to determine taxes.

Taxes incurred. Taxes owed but not yet paid.

Team contract. An agreement developed by the team that defines the guidelines that the team will follow as they work together as a team.

Team process. The process that helps the team work through the stages of team development.

Team leader. A person assigned to manage a team in order to produce a discrete set of deliverables within a project.

Team-based tools. Tools that are specifically designed to enhance team participation and that incorporate the three different sensory learning styles: auditory, visual, and kinesthetic.

Test. The process of checking the outputs of a project against a predetermined set of agreed-on criteria.

Tick size. The specified parameter or its multiple by which the price of a security may vary when trading it at a different price from the last price, whether it be up or down movement from the last price.

Timeline. A length of the entire project, broken down into days, weeks, or months.

Top-down building. Designing a product by constructing a high-level structure and then filling in the gaps in that structure.

Total quality. The management technology that addresses customer focus, prevention, and assurance of quality.

Tracking project progress. The act of determining if the project is on track to meet the commitments outlined in the project plan.

Triple constraint. The three interdependent variables in a project: scope, schedule, and cost.

Undepreciated capital costs. The tax definition of the value of an asset that is eligible for tax depreciation.

Undercapitalization. A situation in which a business does not have sufficient equity in its capital structure.

Unencumbered. Property free and clear of all liens (creditors' secured claims).

Unit variable cost. The specific labor and materials associated with a single unit of goods sold. It does not include general overhead.

Units breakeven. The unit sales volume at which the fixed and variable costs are exactly equal to sales.

Variance. The difference between what occurred and what was planned or projected to occur.

What-if scenarios. Analysis of the economic effect of possible future situations, such as economic downturns, loss of key customers, changes in interest rates or price levels, or new competitors or technologies.

Withdrawn/postponed. From time to time a company will decide that market conditions are out of favor and not conducive to a successful IPO. There are many reasons why a company will decide to withdraw its IPO. Among these reasons are a simple lack of willing investors at that time, market volatility, or the emergence of a bear market.

Work process. A set of steps that produces an output or a deliverable.

Work breakdown structure. A tabular or graphical hierarchical breakdown of the project work into related tasks.

Working capital. The excess of current assets over current liabilities. This represents the amount of net non-fixed assets required in day-to-day operations.

Write-off. A debt that cannot be collected and finally written off as bad. Such a debt is a loss to the company, and the greater the level of bad debts, the less likely an entrepreneur will be able to obtain bank financing. Maintaining bad debts to a minimum is seen as the ability of a company to run efficiently and to have efficient systems in place.

About the Author

Jacques Magliolo is an economist, former director of a stockbroking firm, corporate advisor to multinationals and an international bestselling author of 18 books, including five university MBA textbooks.

Jacques is a specialist in undertaking highly technical economic due diligences, research and feasibility studies on highly complex industries, such a mining, defence force, aviation, astrophysics, chemical, mineral and water related industries.

- Jacques is currently completing his PHD in economics (Stellenbosch University)

Jacques has been an investment and corporate strategist since 1987. He started his career as a financial journalist for the Financial Mail, before being headhunted into stockbroking. Since then he has worked for numerous publications and stockbroking firms, including the Mail & Guardian, UK-based Petroleum Economist and The Star. On the analytical side, Jacques has worked for EW Baldersons, IBCA International, Frankel Pollak Vinderine, CA Miller Raw & Co and Global Capital Securities.

His 30-year experience thus includes stockbroking, business development and corporate strategy. Before setting up his own consultancy in June 2000, he was a director, strategist and head of research for stockbrokers Global Capital Securities.

Index

OTHER TITLES IN THE ENTREPRENEURSHIP AND SMALL BUSINESS MANAGEMENT COLLECTION

Scott Shane, Case Western University, *Editor*

- *Navigating Entrepreneurship: 11 Proven Keys to Success* by Larry Jacobson
- *Global Women in the Start-up World: Conversations in Silicon Valley* by Marta Zucker
- *Understanding the Family Business: Exploring the Differences Between Family and Nonfamily Businesses, Second Edition* by Keanon J. Alderson
- *Growth-Oriented Entrepreneurship* by Alan S. Gutterman
- *Founders* by Alan S. Gutterman
- *Entrepreneurship* by Alan S. Gutterman
- *Sustainable Entrepreneurship* by Alan S. Gutterman
- *Startup Strategy Humor: Democratizing Startup Strategy* by Rajesh K. Pillania
- *The Leadership Development Journey: How Entrepreneurs Develop Leadership Through Their Lifetime* by Jen Vuhuong
- *Getting to Market With Your MVP: How to Achieve Small Business and Entrepreneur Success* by J.C. Baker
- *Can You Run Your Business With Blood, Sweat, and Tears? Volume I: Blood* by Stephen Elkins-Jarrett and Nick Skinner
- *Can You Run Your Business With Blood, Sweat, and Tears? Volume II: Sweat* by Stephen Elkins-Jarrett and Nick Skinner
- *Can You Run Your Business With Blood, Sweat, and Tears? Volume III: Tear* by Stephen Elkins-Jarrett and Nick Skinner
- *Family Business Governance: Increasing Business Effectiveness and Professionalism* by Keanon J. Alderson
- *Department of Startup: Why Every Fortune 500 Should Have One* by Ivan Yong Wei Kit and Sam Lee

Announcing the Business Expert Press Digital Library

Concise e-books business students need for classroom and research

This book can also be purchased in an e-book collection by your library as

- a one-time purchase,
- that is owned forever,
- allows for simultaneous readers,
- has no restrictions on printing, and
- can be downloaded as PDFs from within the library community.

Our digital library collections are a great solution to beat the rising cost of textbooks. E-books can be loaded into their course management systems or onto students' e-book readers.

The **Business Expert Press** digital libraries are very affordable, with no obligation to buy in future years. For more information, please visit **www.businessexpertpress.com/librarians**. To set up a trial in the United States, please email **sales@businessexpertpress.com**.

www.ingramcontent.com/pod-product-compliance
Lightning Source LLC
Chambersburg PA
CBHW061306220326
41599CB00026B/4749